EAVAN BOLAND, LISEL MUELLER, SAPPHO, WISLAWA SZYM-
BORSKA, EMILY DICKINSON, CHARLOTTE MEW, ANNA
AKHMATOVA, KATALIN LADIK, CATHY SMITH BOWERS, KATH-
RYN STRIPLING BYER, JIMMIE MARGARET GILLIAM, JANICE
MOORE FULLER, PAT RIVIERE-SEEL, MAYA ANGELOU, SHA-
RON OLDS, SYLVIA PLATH, ADRIENNE RICH, JUDY GRAHN,
LINDA GREGG, MARIE HOWE, ELLEN BRYANT VOIGHT,
HEATHER McHUGH, EDNA ST VINCENT MILLAY, ELIZABETH
BISHOP, H.D., ELENI FORTUNI, DERORA BERNSTEIN, DO-
REEN STOCK, TESS GALLAGHER, NELLY SACHS, CAROL LEE
SANCHEZ, PAULA GUN ALLEN, MARGE PIERCY, CAROLYN
FORCHÉ, GWENDOLYN BROOKS, DENISE LEVERTOV, NIKKI
GIOVANNI, MARY OLIVER, RUTH STONE, HONOR MOORE, MI-
RABAI, MARYLIN HACKER, CHRISTINA ROSETTI, JUNE JOR-
DAN, bel hooks, STEVIE SMITH, DARA WIER, GERTRUDE STEIN

"Inspired and inspiring. The poems in this collection illustrate the transformative power of imagination. They bring vibrant energy to words the women speak."

–bell hooks, writer and cultural critic, author of many books, *Belonging; A Culture of Place*, forthcoming new poems *Appalachian Elegy* and a new book of essays *Writing Beyond Race*.

"There is no doubt that readers will remember these poems, because *Remember Me as a Time of Day* is full of hauntings and transformations, arduous journeys and transcendent joys. And, like the *Book of Hours* that its title intimates, this collection marks time with intricate measures wrought by twelve poets "bending the world with their words"—Alicia Valbuena, Barbara Gravelle, Eileen Walkenstein, Emöke B'Rácz, Genie Joiner, Maryann Jennings, Nancy Sanders, Patricia Harvey, Piri B'Rácz Gibson, Sena Rippel, Virginia Haynes Redfield and Zoe Durga Harber—each excavating buried histories, quiet triumphs, and complicated redemptions."

–Holly Iglesias, author of *Angels of Approach* and *Souvenirs of a Shrunken World*

Remember Me as a Time of Day

Poetry By

Alicia Valbuena

Barbara Gravelle

Eileen Walkenstein

Emöke B'Rácz

Genie Joiner

Maryann Jennings

Nancy Sanders

Patricia Harvey

Piri B'Rácz Gibson

Sena Rippel

Virginia Haynes Redfield

Zoe Durga Harber

Burning Bush Press of Asheville

Published by Burning Bush Press of Asheville,
a division of Renaissance Bookfarm, Inc.
Inquiries to Malaprop's Bookstore/Cafe
55 Haywood St., Asheville, NC 28801
www.malaprops.com

Printed in the United States of America
Cover illustration by Emöke B'Rácz
Interior illustrations by Piri B'Rácz Gibson
Design by Kasey Gruen

ISBN-13: 978-09848308-5-5

Introduction

Remember Me as a Time of Day is the work of "Women on Words" —twelve writers living in the mountains in and around Asheville, NC. Like the poetry circles that preceded them, they differ widely in age, background and education, and they meet regularly at the now legendary Malaprop's Bookstore/Cafe in downtown Asheville. What binds these women together is their reverence for the individual human voice, and the opportunity to express themselves. The poems have been grouped by the poet, providing a view into the process and soul of each writer. All the poets journeyed and arrived in Asheville with a personal commitment to writing, while Emöke B'Rácz, founder of Malaprop's and Downtown Books & News, made her own commitment to the bookstore, women writing, and poetry.

Remember Me as a Time of Day joyfully celebrates the thirtieth anniversary of Malaprop's Bookstore/Cafe, which has long offered safe haven to writers, regional and national, and an open forum to voice their ideas. But neither the bookstore, "Women on Words", or this anthology would be possible without the efforts of Emöke. In 1982, this young Hungarian immigrant pulled together the money to rent a small space in downtown Asheville, a risky area in serious decline at the time. The story of the new bookstore's undeniable role in revitalizing downtown Asheville is known by many, as is the spirit and determination of Emöke, who built an outstanding independent bookstore/cafe and opened doors to writers and the community. Diversity in writing and representation of authors has been a remarkable achievement for our small community. The poets of W.O.W. are grateful to Emöke and the award-winning Malaprop's for bringing prosperity of mind to the community.

Contents

Alicia

sometimes he swims

Alicia Valbuena enjoys writing poetry, swimming in oceans, climbing mountains, looking at art, and learning new things. She is not sure what

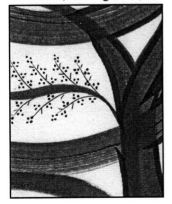

her life's passion is yet, but knows it must be principally concerned with aesthetics. Before moving to Asheville she studied literature in south Florida, and even before that she built forts in her basement during Connecticut winters so she could read for hours without being bothered. There is so much Alicia wants to do, often times she does not know where to begin.

1

it was written

my mom didn't think she'd survive
when she miscarried that night,
alone on the couch,
underneath blue glow
from the television.

I would have been a boy
three months later–
if so it was written.
but it wasn't:
it was 1983. winter. the trees
bare. the snow only an inch and
already frozen. the dead
world was not ready
to embrace
something new.

I didn't realize until
last summer that
it was me that night–a boy,
very much alive
inside her–
and that by receding,
transposing myself
into blood and tissue to be
poured out,
I was like the tahina tree,
that only blooms once
in a hundred years
and not until the time
is exactly right.

make her cry

1. she remembers being two–
the day you and john scanlon
built her swing set. it was brand
new wood: one swing, one slide,
and monkey bars.

2. you were always joking
around–
an old picture shows you
and john in matching shirts, six
pockets on each, lined up like
windows on an apartment building.
you are wearing those plastic
glasses with the attached nose
and mustache. yours doesn't
fit well over your own black walrus.

3. she once read in
her mom's journal
about the wonderful faces
she made as a newborn
when you kissed her forehead,
cheeks.

4. there are beers in hands in the picture,
cigars in mouths. she used to feel
scared and worried whenever
you lit your cigar. she did not understand
its thick smoke.

5. she remembers
when you began to build her
swing set, because back then,
you really had to build them–

get the hammer, saw,
sweat in the new may sun, all
for you daughter, two,
watching from the sliding door–
you have to build it because
she will grow up,
mature to a woman someday,
have her own house and cat.
she will move away
and never ask you for help
or steal bites from your dinner plate.

6. you may feel like you never had a daughter
at times.
she will prove her autonomy.
but none of this matters now
because she will always
remember when you began
to build her swing set.
twenty-three years ago you leaned the ladder
for her slide against the tree,
laughed, said all done! and walked
a few steps toward her.
and that was enough to make her cry.

this is how

the night comes through the screen door
when you are four feet tall.
when all you have to worry about
is in your dreams. this is how
the night comes,
when you wait and wait, not blinking
for fear of missing
the migration from light to dark.
this is how the night comes,
like people whispering in the hallway
long after bed.

remember me as a time of day

that summer, when everything was infinite and eternal,
when the hot connecticut sun sent you out
barefoot and blonde in the morning–
you and I were together almost every day.

I would wake to the disappearing tips
of your golden waves as the sun pushed its way from behind leaves,
silhouetting each one separately
against the orange sky.
I would wake to the flying hem of your transparent dress–
your body floating weightlessly away from me,
through wild grass, the way cotton dances
in june air.

each morning I would wake, my eyes chasing you, your eyes chasing
the sun. I admired every bend of your knee,
envied every tunnel of light
sent through the small cracks–
through the thin slits between your fingers,
through the soft points where your arms, thin as bottles,
meet your shoulders.
the sun shining through the delicate skin that covers your legs where
they join
to your fourteen-year-old hips.

at the top of the hill,
you would fall and roll onto your back, like a happy cat, as if
surrendering–
realizing you were not going to catch
the sun, but thankful for the chase.

at these moments I longed to be the grass
that held your body
in its body–

so perfect and still were each in the morning's fresh light.
I often dreamt of you
knocking on my window–
lightly tapping with curled fingers
until I rose from bed and slid open the glass, hot with your breath.
I imagined you leaning in closely, whispering so softly in my ear
I have to strain to hear the words–
remember me always,
as a time of day.

dissoluto (or bullfrog)

when you put
a bullfrog in water
it is happy.
because
water is life
and the
frog's desire
is like all of ours–
to live
in the water
buried
in cool mud,
exercising
our lungs
for all the world
to hear.
when you put
a bullfrog in water
it (or he or she)
is thankful. as
we all are thankful
to sip at our first
thirst,
to get dirt under
our fingernails,
to roll down
a grassy hill
on a sunny
afternoon.

coniunctio (or hat)

a hat and love–
a hat as a motif
of a love,
a hat as a symbol
of the lightness
when first
meeting a love.
where would
the love be
if the hat wasn't?
they
would not have
shared time
in front of the mirror,
she
in underwear,
him
in pants
and tie–

they could not
have passed
the hat
and known.

erase
the hat
and she would
never have
stayed,
never have
been
so intrigued.

separato (or apricot)

skin
flesh
pit.
or soul
or heart
or nucleus
(if you
want to be
scientific).
skin,
the membrane–
delicate,
easily punctured
by knives,
scissors,
glass,
teeth.

flesh–
delicious
inside.
lasts
longer than skin.

bone
is all
that will be
left
one day.
finally,

the center.
the core.
not

too large
but large
enough
for new life.
not molten
lava or even
hot. it just is–
vital,
effervescent,
ready
to be
recycled.

florida nights

you used to sing in the morning, and I'll admit,
I loved waking to the sound of the shower falling
on matted dreads
and the smell
of fried plantains and mangoes served hot
over light morning dub
from the cd player.

I'll admit, I fell in love on the first night–
you asked if I wanted to go for a run on the beach,
fearing I wouldn't keep up with your long legs,
we rode bikes.
over palmetto bridge and through the spanish river tunnels.
you suggested we have our first kiss,
but still laughed
when I dropped my bike and pressed my hands to the back
of your warm neck.

we rode back quietly, perfectly,
the empty night streets giving the illusion
we were the only ones
in the world.

a joint and cup of fruit punch later
you kissed me again.
you took my shirt off and held my arms
above my head–
my beaded necklace still in place between my breasts.

love is fire

sitting on the porch at night you watch her
light the corners of her unused dinner napkin
before tossing it over the banister.
this makes you nervous. she knows it does–
she has loved you for a long time.
but love is fire
and like the night, it never lasts.

or else be generous

sometimes, I like to watch my neighbor annie. she is a quiet lady, walks
with her head down. some may call her an 'odd bird,' but that makes
me think of a goose, or some other long-necked animal with glasses,
maybe a pearl necklace. so I prefer to remain enchanted by her sudden
and frequent bike rides, her conversations with the black cat with the
white paws. sometimes I see the cat waiting in the oak tree in her yard.
he sits between two heavy branches and stares across the short street
into our window. he looks bluntly into my eyes. I took a picture one day
so I will never forget how it feels to have an animal judge every cell
in your body and then forget and walk away and love you anyway. my
neighbor is a good ping pong player. good, not great, but good enough
to hold her own at the bar at the end of the road during their wednesday
tournament, where the winner wins no tangible thing like a trophy, but
instead gets a bar tab–expected to either get too drunk and walk home,
or else be generous. annie, I imagine, would choose the latter, but this
is all hypothetical, except for this last part: once I found a note on the
ground where her driveway connects to the road– "would it embarrass
you very much if I were to tell you I love you?"

gardening at seventy

my sunscreened shoulders are two melting scoops
of vanilla ice cream. my old knees, brown
clam shells in the dirt.

in a moment a quiet car will roll down my driveway
and I will ask the strangers if they are day lily collectors.
they will smile as they shake their pretty heads and laugh,
the young girl's red skirt really standing out
against all this green.

downtown

that afternoon we got drunk
off five dollar mojitos–the wednesday special–
and walked around town.
we stopped by the emporium for a gift to give
your grandmother for her seventy-fifth next week–
after shallowly eyeing some glass-topped tables and,
until our stomachs ached, smelling all twenty-six
fragrances of soap, we found the hand–
a giant hand made of oak,
the tips of its index finger and thumb pushed lightly
together, offering wisdom.
on sale for $995
a tag read–

halfway to the counter where a lady sat,
her hair a tight ball, lips pursed like she had just tasted
something sour. a queen in her castle she scorns with
disinterest a newspaper and flips the page, hardly touching it, as if
throwing something away. halfway to the counter
I ask her, my breath reminiscent of rum
and sugar, my right arm extended, finger
pointing like a child,
how many trees did it take
to make this hand of shiva?

I walk away
satisfied
by her right to remain silent.
we should do this more often
you say. and I agree–
the september air an aphrodisiac, my head
ethereal and light.

driving home

driving home along nightingale road I am
suddenly so grateful
I exist.
maybe the limoncello is to blame, or
the dirty talk, or
the recent certitude that my cheeks
still maintain their ability to turn bright red
when everyone is watching– or maybe
its the way he holds me,
in the backseat of his parents' grand prix–
him, ear pressed against the window, arm wedged between my hip
and casserole dish. (earlier, the moment I felt like an adult for the first
time
in twenty-two years–
when I reclaimed the empty dish and left–
it's touch solid and cold against my breast,
like a football whose capture
I greatly deserved).

driving home along nightingale road I am
suddenly so grateful–
a stomach full of liquor, but
I am a child
curled up in the safety of a backseat,
keeping an eye through my window on the thin slice of stars–
millions and millions of light years away.

love poem before bed

if your face were a small town somewhere,
I imagine it would be a place
I'd like to visit, maybe live.
in the winter I could ski one of the many trails
down your nose.
the black diamond would be too difficult,
the blue square, just right.
the café that would sit at the small summit
where the center of your upper lip ascends just a tiny bit
would serve Russian roulette lattes and creme brule
cappuccinos, and would never
charge more for soy milk
instead of cream.

where the snowy mountains end
and the forest begins would be located
down your impeccable jaw.
the forest would be a mecca for campers and backpackers, and
even I would entertain a walk in the woods from time
to time, if it weren't for fear of getting lost
in the jaunty tangles.
sure, there are parts where the trees
are thinned out and you can see the stars
on a clear night, but as I always assure you,
it is only a matter of time before
they fill in.
just be patient.

yes, life would be perfect
on your face, I imagine.
as long as you don't sneeze,
and the soft opulence of your lips–
the softest I have ever felt,
remains something we can rely on.

my partner and I are on the old road to the sea.

his footprints follow
mine– erasing mine.
he is a mountain
man, has never
tasted salt on his lips.

he charts the
new land, mapping
his way– the first:
sailing from one
beach to another, alone.
salt and barnacles cling
to the wood of
his modest boat like
a man clings
to his mate at night.

sometimes
he swims.

he loves the
feeling– the
invariant way
of the sea,
her molecules
bursting all at once
against his dark skin.

I have made it to
the water by now,
and am floating, eyes
closed. but
my partner
is still at sea–

where I do not exist.
where I am merely matter,
some force of energy rolling
with the waves
that knock his boat.

of anticipation

I
this poem is why I can't sleep at night why I can't lay my head
to rest when there is all this corruption in the world this poem
is what keeps my eyes wide and mind restless long after the moon is hung
our world is coming to a dead end your dollar no
longer means anything to the man at the gas station you
will need five more of those if you want anything from him
this poem is addressing those who sit comfortably
on their pedestals
why am I down here? catching
the raining coins that hit my head and stick in my throat
I know what they speak of and yet
I am guilty too
we all are guilty
why do we give what little money we have to condemned
institutions? why do we throw our money to the factories where
animals are killed
why do we throw our money to Hollywood just to save a seat
in a dirty theater where we witness destruction
in fashion of the latest blockbluster
why—when I am worthless when we all are worthless
when nothing means a thing and yet it means everything
why am I so little and so powerless? why do I waste
my time awake at night only questioning and
not answering?

II
this poem is the day that I wake
this poem is the day that we all wake to our
world our lives our society when we all wake to ourselves and
finally
for the first time in our existences become conscious
when we no longer are receivers and killers but givers
givers of life and liberation

22

peace fulfillment independence I want to be the one to rise above all
the sleepers and pave way to enlightenment
I want I need to be pure when even
the whitest dove is covered in the blackest of soot I want
to listen to the stories in the music I hear and see and taste and become
and to feel the earth beneath my feet as natural as it once was
I want to listen to those minds that preached
awareness through art through love and compassion through
psychedelics
who warned us about the evils of conformity
they told us to rise against and what have I done here
sitting on the floor at night
alone
in my head

III
this poem has a heartbeat
like you and me it lies awake wondering
asking contemplating hoping seeking praying of ways
biting chewing digesting ideas
to save the planet one beat or one footprint or one song at a time
to sustain our face
because once truly is not enough
begging ways to discover energy love light awareness truth beauty and
to discover
fulfillment and what keeps you from that place in your dreams
this poem is to all of us awake in the darkness
awake but sleeping
this poem is anger and hope packaged tightly onto a single red petal
in that lost garden
compressed and ready to shatter
this poem is the calm before the storm
the calm when the sky has silenced its creatures and the trees stand in
perfect tranquility

when the world has quieted its desires and the only sound is that of
anticipation
this poem will someday put me to sleep
but not until my mind is fully conscious and I have become
the change that will flourish
the change that will invade and nourish and nurture and feed and
progress when
you I him her us all of us are awake and powerful
this poem is the day our lives begin

for you

love is the day I last saw you.
you had on your plastic pearl necklace
and your trademark red lipstick.
your hair was curled, leaving
long forgotten burns on your neck.
you took my hand in yours and I knew
what was coming.
I have been waiting for you
you said.

(for Mary Desilets, 1915-2009)

you used to tell us about the music you heard

we knew
it was all in your head
but still agreed,
nodded,
told you it was as beautiful.

the day you
started stealing
newspapers
from the woman
across the hall
was the beginning
of the end.
there was nothing
for us to do
but wait.
outside the rain fell
softly,
steadily.
the birds stopped
coming by
your window.
they too,
knew.

but the music
still carried on
as loud as
ever.

june

on the ninth he handed us
your pearl necklace
and your
wedding ring,
tight and neat
in a little bag.

on the sixth you turned off
your alarm clock,
folded your clothes,
organized your papers–
old letters,
crossword puzzles,
opened your window.
and on the seventh,

in the early morning
before the sun
you flew out
and up.

twelfth,
all the seats
were filled–I
finally felt
tears
hitting
my lips.

my mom has your hands,
your wrists,
ears,
skin,
eyes

memorial poem

it has been one
year–
I am still with him
in a new house, city.
you are still there–
it's hot again. the cat
is gone
and so are the
sunflowers–
neither
could be
without her.
sometimes
I wonder
how
I can be

without the
extra muffins
stolen from the
dining hall
or a pocketful
of plastic
bangles.

I just realized
why I can't write
too well. The
table is too
high

or I am too
short.

now
I will finish
with love.

Barbara

The Gypsy Dancing

Barbara Gravelle's poetry has appeared in many journals and anthologies. The list includes *The New Orleans Review of Literature*, Loyola University Press; *Mosaic, A Journal for The Comparative Study of Lit-*

erature and Ideas, University of Manitoba Press; *Moving to Antarctica*, edited by Margaret Kaminski for Dust Books, Paradise, CA; and *Contemporary Women Poets*, edited by Jennifer McDowell and M. Loventhal, Merlin Press, San Jose, CA. Barbara has published four books of poetry, the most recent of which is *Poet on the Roof of The World: The Kythera Poems*, Archangel Books, Asheville, NC 2010.

For Vadim Bora

I

Thank you for Estair, Lucy and Caspar,
the bronze cats on the prowl at Wall Street.
Also for the rat and the mouse. All the
sculptures and the paintings you have left as mementoes,
your presence, for as long as you could stay.

I had hoped for a sculpture of Zelda Fitzgerald, revealing the
enigma of her generation, the women who married writers.

A great work that would tell of the strength of your genius,
a life-sized Bronze, someone I could talk to,
standing in fourth position somewhere near trees, the
consummate flapper, the Southern Belle,
only my dream now. Vadim Bora, you have left us.

II

I raise my glass of red wine to your spirit, a little boy walks
across the steps of the Caucasus. Vadim Bora you were charming
as I sat with the Greek and the singer dinking wine, hearing your
story, and watching your brown eyes laughing.
A conversation indelible now. Vadim Bora, you were charming.

I dreamed I kept missing your memorial as I carried a plastic
bag of vibrant hand-crafted glass platters. They had sharp edges
like the secret gypsy I am.
I wanted your clothes, dying
to try them, when a shimmering black robe lured me into it. The robe
lifted me off the floor and we slowly rose toward the ceiling.
If I never get back down – I want you to sculpt ME in the midnight
where the corner of the room converges with the ceiling.
Never mind Zelda Fitzgerald.

Dec. 1 Evening

Sitting by the wood-burning stove
at Ray's place in Leicester, a horned
crystal moon is rising.
A winter night crisp and quiet is
slowly falling. Over the candle-lighted
dinner I am already drowsy.
And then sweet sleep –
merle blue Ciel, sleeping by my bed.

In the early morning, not at all awake
I put on my shoes to answer nature's
insistent call. Ciel, Australian Shepherd
with the one blue eye, herds me into
the dark. Barking, she establishes
a perimeter of protection around me.
As in the chill morning frost,
Orion, Ursa Minor and Cassiopeia
twinkle above me.

Morning 1950

I creep out from under warm blankets,
pull on my boots and throw on my
winter coat over my pajamas.
I slip out the back door
into the panoramic gray dawn.
A strong sun cuts through salmon
and purple-colored clouds. It is as if
a stage curtain has danced open on
its pulley – the sun breaks through, a bird calls.
This is my moment, stolen away from
sleeping parents, my siblings,
even the cat wants to stay by the
banked coals of the fire.
It's just me and this sunrise,
with the scent of balsam fir.

Grandmother Fire

"When you do something
you should burn yourself completely
like a good bonfire leaving no trace
of yourself."
Shuryu Suzuki Roshi

She sits at the point where
two ancient rivers meet,
in a current running through
a virgin forest. She sizzles and her
body heat makes fog.

The primitive comforts her.
She knows she has not lost
her wild sense of smell,
even a faint scent
will tell her how long ago
a predator passed by.

She still has the skills
that have saved her kind
for generations.
She watches her granddaughter
who drifts and spins
like a new leaf
fallen in the current.

Unforgotten instincts tell her
another came here not long before
to challenge her water place.
She knows the scent of that
menstrual blood, thrown out like
a threat.

In another season that one will
leave behind the softer smell
of mother's milk – produced on cue
for a newborn.

Grandmother Fire, so long on this earth,
is already named among the distant stars.
She knows this small vulnerable planet
could disappear.

And I, granddaughter many times
descended from the one watched,
spinning and drifting in the old river,
have meditated long on Grandmother Fire.

I move in closer to the fire in
the center of the circle of dancers.
As I reach toward the fire
her strong smooth big-knuckled hand
comes out of the flames and clasps mine.
I remember the feel of grandmother's
hands, two small falcons. As she takes
me into her wisdom body, the stress of
clinging to my corporeal form subsides.

Ah, before me,
She is Unelanuhi, She is Shakti,
Ha Om Tare Tam So Ha
She is Righed Drolma
She is grandmother star
She is grandmother fire
Give her your flesh and she will
transmit it to pure white ash.

Pastoral: Poem found at Willow Cove

White buoyant clouds
float through the so blue sky.
Sheep are grazing here and there
on grass green meadows and up
the rolling hill pastures
of Willow Cove.

Some are bah – bah – baaaahing
about me asking personified questions.
"Who is she – bah?
What is she doing in our pasture?
She doesn't look like a Little Bo Peep
at all! baaaaaaaaah!"

Over the sound of rushing creek water
the solitary Pilgrim gander
squawks, proclaiming
"Once I had a mother goose
but she died – then I fell in love
with a sheep and she died – ah me,"
He waddles and struts. "What to do –
What to do – lost my goose –
lost my sheep – lost my ewe,"

I have hiked up the hill
to a round granite rock
that sits imposingly under
a laden red apple tree which
leans like an awning.
I heft my body up and then over
the rock's contours till I sit in a
moss-covered crevice.

Jack and Jill, the large White Great Pyrenees
sheep dogs have climbed up to sit with me.
One on each side
Peace in this meadow
they nudge their big soft happy
faces against my hair and come
together enveloping me in white fur.
Such silken warmth – these elegant
working dogs
cleverly protecting their sheep
while tussling me.

We sit three synchronized blithe spirits
and watch the black and golden butterflies
and bumble bees sip nectar from the blue
scotch thistle flower. White puffs of
thistle rise up like sprites on the pure air.

A steady long bleat comes over the
the forest's perimeter –
Jack and Jill shoot off fast as
arrows straight toward the sound,
and I am left, alone, under the
apple tree.

Ask Alice, When She's Ten Feet Tall

I've been down in this rabbit hole so long
I feel I have become the positive in the
negative space of it. Maybe it's my grave
and I'm already dead.

However, if I squint, I can still see light
out of the corner of my left eye, the light
at the end of the rabbit hole, that is.

Earlier, a great old Indian just came by
said his name was "Don Juan"
said he had some advice on getting out of
rabbit holes, said, " he thought I was going
too far for one little episode in a memoir,
or for possible other creative non-fiction."
He said, "Writing should not be a literary
exercise, said, " it should to be an exercise
in sorcery."

"What do you mean?" I asked.
He said, "Get yourself out of the rabbit
hole, and I'll tell you the rest." I heard
him walk on.

In a little while the rabbit formerly known
as B'rer came by. He wanted to rent the
rabbit hole. I said, "Look Rabbit, you can
have it, if I can just get out of it!" B'rer
went off - but soon came back with a large jar.
" I brought you some Bear Grease, " he said.
"Try to rub it all over you and maybe you
can slip out."

I did and it worked! I am
like the earth goddess reborn into
broad daylight. When my legs
uncramped and I could move my head
on my neck, I looked into the distance
and saw the old wise slow Yaqui...
I took out after him in a run.

Mountain Mamas

So having nothing better
that weekend, I took you

to the Gold Country on Route 49.
To my special and secret lair,
a picturesque inn from the days
of the gold miners, the 1849ers.

You did not love me.
You told me that.
But, "because the sex
was off the scale and you
did love to wear my red silk
and lace Italian panties,
there was no good reason
to let all *that* go just yet."

So you said over a Placerville
Hang Town breakfast, fried
oysters and eggs. As served to
condemned historical desperados,
you were pouting, you punk
Russian. My heart-break mistake
Mikhail Baryshnikov look-alike.

So I left the western movie
saloon décor to ponder
and primp in the powder room.
Then with much loud jingle jangle
the real show came in.

From my 45
degree angle I saw ten or more
leg bands of small silver bells
stretched over remarkable cowgirl boots.
I came out. They kept jangling,
big women in Stetson hats
as if in answer to my unarticulated
"What the . . ." their red tee shirts
read "Mountain Mamas."

It was a large dream motorcycle
rescue. I didn't stop to think,
just grabbed my purse. I was outa'
there. "Catch ya later Mikhail."
All the way to Berkeley, I rode
 with the Mamas, behind Rare Ruby.
This was 'something' better on a dusty
trail to joy.

Added-Americana

When Giovanni Phillipo Soso
landed on Ellis Island and went
through the immigration process,
he stepped sprightly over the litter
of all those dropped suffixes.
He was destined to be
above the fray.

There was no surname suffix
to be lopped off, but the
intake officer copying his name
from the suitcase tag accidentally
added USA,
the arrived-at destination
and Giovanni Phillipo Soso
became John Phillip Sousa.
Hence a musical icon, the sousaphone
and many future spirited marches
composed for patriotic holidays.

Ariea

You were the illusive alchemical word,
the key to the magic box lock
I, the woman word warrior
chased you vertically
chased you horizontally –
dug through layers of onion skin
in the Oxford unabridged –
and finally found you at last
hiding like a red fox
curled in a ram's horn.

Areia, adjective – derived from
the mighty war god Aries.
Epinome also for Aphrodite Ariea.
She, who according to Deomosthenes,
at Nestor's banquet table, "was caught
in the golden net crafted by, her so called
husband, Hephaestus, a Goldsmith.
Snared with her lover Aries – in flagrante
dilicto.

Aphrodite, who could hold her own
with the pre-Homeric bronze sword,
but chose to be seduced by what waited
under his golden Hellenic kilt.

O Aries – O Ariea
caught! Mainly because she wanted to
look into his gold war shield –
it made such a sassy mirror for her
to gaze at her own glowing reflection.

Mycenae

The last thing we heard
that night was the wind
howling like a mad woman
up the stairwell of the Hotel
Clytemnestra.

Before morning, the wind
had died down.
The first thing we heard
when we awoke was
de-ka-oc-toe the call of
the Decaoctura, throaty
like the dove, announcing
the date spot-on; it was
the eighteenth of October.
Always that call on the same date,
so we were told by the Greeks,
who vowed they always heard those
birds on their migrating way to Libya
on the eighteenth day of that month.

Then our last hike in an ancient
place, distant goat bells on the
triangle mountain that you see
through the Lion Gate.
Now shrouded by fog
we tramp on till we break through
into sunlight – bidding Mycenae adieu,
boarding the train and all-too-soon

I am on the hydrofoil going back to
the island. You are on the pier with
arms up raised to the goddess – growing
smaller, the sun still gleaming in your
cropped golden hair.

Premonition

1. Strophe

It was years before anyone would
recognize the skeletal shape
in the sand at Limmni
but the persistent tides
eroding the bank slowly
exposed
the strata of shards
and finally, the human skull.

You and I are swimming
not knowing up from down
inside the immense tidal wave
that took us in a past life.
Bedraggled, mouth open
lungs clawing for air
I break the surface,
but in this racing nightmare
I was swallowing the black smoke
of volcanic ash. I could neither
breathe nor see the shore.

2. Greek Tragedy

To show your disdain at my rejection
you swept up a woman in the taverna.
A blond child clinging to her hips
was crying, and holding on from behind,
It was a failed
tango.

I danced a defiant women's line dance
with two sympathetic village supporters.
Maria, scornfully leading the line, then Anna,
who knew of betrayals, then me trying to
once and for all shake you loose.

The sea demon of Cavo Meleas would not
let you off the island. Oh, the irreversible acts
of that sea god—days stranded, when
we waited for the storm to end
so the boat from Athens could land.

3. Antistrophe

The sea that brought you was the same sea
that took you away and with you the pathos
in your patterns of reaction; my wave of nausea
in the wake that followed. The ferryboat
filling up, listing over and sinking –
all souls miraculously saved.

Then on a silent morning
no sound, even the waves quiet
in a rose streaked dawn with that small
star setting at the point where the sky begins.

I was that waking woman survivor –
panting on the pebble beach, seeing history
recur – sensing the strength of the ancients
who had watched from the shore until
the Mycenaean invasions began
and the Island was on fire.

They Want Their Clothes Back

The dead Gypsies want their clothes back. O
the beauty – the beauty of the specters – these
long – tall – drop-dead gorgeous – definitely
disaffected – stone cold – dead Gypsies want
their clothes back.
Sure their eyes are green.
Even their dead eyes are green.
What's this? I can't help but ask.
The night of the Living Dead Gypsies?
And do I really have to give them
their clothes back?

Their feet keep moving as though the instinct
to keep stepping hasn't died.
More and more dead Gypsies join the march.
The dead Gypsies are coming and
they want their clothes back.

They are on the move in the wind.
These were the living Detroit gypsies who
told fortunes in storefronts on Cherry St.

Now dead children who danced beside
Highway 70's over pass. While the Clinchfield
Mill workers threw coins to them.

The family – of whom my Balladeer Grandpa Doc
warned me. "Why they'd snatch that
little red coat off you so fast you wouldn't
see it vanish." The one that on Othos Paleologos
made my off-white raw silk suit coat disappear.

The group in the van at Karithiadika
who managed to get the keys to the
house where I was staying and left town.
Every day after that I had to crawl
in through a tiny stone-framed window.

The dead Gypsies of the south of France
who hold sacred the body, glowing in her
tomb, of the black saint Sara, also known as
the daughter of Jesus.

They have come to worship
the black Madonna of Les Maries de la Mer,
likewise the Magdalene whose skull graces
the monastery at St. Baum and because
Biblical history just can't get it right – they
were either called prostitutes or Maria.
Tell me. Who can resist a dancing Gypsy
with a marigold behind his ear?
The truth is, I don't even know where
their clothes are.

The Gypsy Dancing

What did she care?
She wore her mortality
like a scarf
that slipped down
over a sly shoulder
and as she danced
in the shadows
drifted to expose

one nut brown breast.
What did she care
if she ceased to exist,
deceased?
The scarf – dark blue
and transparent edged
with tiny gold coins
if not already lost
would be tossed

a splash
of dark blue
in the bottom of
the chest, among
other colors and their
sheer fabric myths
all told and final
danced on a violin's
last vibrato sigh.

This scarf
that embraced her
drumming heart, held her
moist heat close and moved
on the air like a quivering flame
over her head and down her
sacred body, to fall at her
holy feet, would be dead
as a shroud in a wooden trunk
containing clothing belonging
to an illusive Romany woman.

What did she care?
What did she care?
She was in the wind.
She was the east wind.

And did she care?
I think she did not.

Night of the Black Suckling Piglet

Suddenly in the midst of life Tommy
puts a small black piglet in my arms.
I think of Alice B and the small black pigs
of, was it Sicily? And of the ones sacrificed
by Demeter at Eleusis, to bring her errant
wandering, abducted daughter back.
Bits or Snort, name not settled yet, snorts.
I snort it a message, it responds.
It said: "Hey
I can read Arabic,
those words you refuse to reveal
tattooed on your back
say – y'all can kiss my cute little asterisk."

That was the night the lioness caught you
in something of a rude embrace, her weighty
claws combing – her hungry eyeball sucking –
the same summer night the piglet com-
municated the meaning of the secret universe.

The night I decided that all my prophecies,
reflections, my deep-thoughts, great ideas
would only be revealed to beasts – now that I
could speak animal so fluently – that night
I decided to stop talking to people.

Already I am a cult object with sincere devotees
who have set about to learn the animal
vernacular. Little do they know that they are

setting themselves up to be eaten by piglets.
Hey after Gaza, Tunisia—then Morocco?
I am certain the myth is in danger of being
mauled and mangled, so I'm getting outa' here.

Eileen

Passion Knows No Propriety

Eileen has written poems all her life. Many of these she still carries in her head and will "perform" them when asked. She is enamored of Shakespeare and has acted in some of his plays, most recently "Henry V" with the Montford Park Players in Asheville. Her published books include: *Fat Chance; Don't Shrink to Fit!; Beyond the Couch; Your Inner Therapist; The Imprinters. Fat Chance* was  published in Italy in translation under the title: *Behind the Mask / The Secret Lives of the Food-Obsessed.* Eileen also wrote, produced and performed in "The Theatre of the Obsessed," a multimedia theatre piece about addictions and obsessions which includes audience participation. It was presented in Rome and Naples, Italy and in Philadelphia and New York.

Passion Knows No Propriety

Passion knows no propriety:
no "pardon me" or "if you please,"
no "coulds" or "woulds" or "shoulds" to tease…
its one concern—*SATIETY*.
Passion knows no delicacy:
no shallow breath that comes to tea
to balance life upon its knee
so carefully…so-o-o-o c-a-r-e-f-u-l-l-y.
Passion knows no security:
no civilized maturity
with pros and cons of consequences.
A leaper!—not sitter on fences.
Passion knows no style or fashion:
no Sciaparelli or St. Clare;
in fact, would rather have you bare—
Passion follows only Passion.
So when, after due c-o-n-s-i-d-e-r-a-t-i-on,
with m-e-a-s-u-r-e-d breath, dressed properly,
you finally decide to come to tea:
you
   won't
      find
         me!

On First Seeing Michelangelo's Moses
(San Pietro in Vincoli, Rome)

Heavily was seated on that frowned brow
the stern command,
lofty and thunderous:
That I heard mountains break and seas stand still.
The full-veined hand, resting in power,
held might to crush a world
or to construct a universe.
The chains of muscles undulated over that
seated form:
That I heard the cries of a multitude enslaved
or a whole race set free.
But most: the fierce eyes pinned me, kneeling,
to an infinitesimal space,
The while my soul soared with the soft-singing
angels of mercy.

To begin before sin again!

To begin before sin and fig leaf
long before the fall
when the mind sees all
with the eyes still blind.
I have seen too much sin:
bloated bodies, purple, asleep on grates
in passageways,
Yoricks in mass graves,
girls with wild eyes and abandoned trust
wearing stigmata of their fathers' lust;
electrocution chairs sanctified: sit ye down
sit ye down
an eye for an eye ye know
While my eye, saturate, trained not to cry.
Unshed tears fall behind the eye,
surround the heart,
freeze,
teach to look at all sights colder,
to unremember,
Soon I shall forget
I ever cried for my grandmother.

Advice to a Lover from an Old Man

Ah Lad -
whose arms, though charred,
yet, yet, reach yearning,
whose heart though scarred
by her, keeps burning;
reach, reach, nor cease
despite her spurning:
Love's wisdom you
by this are learning.
Once I, like you,
a maiden cherished;
but pride was King:
thence all love perished.
And now my arms,
intact and free,
alone embrace
my idiocy.

I'll Stay Home with the Boys

(For the Falkland Islands or wherever,
for Prime Minister Thatcher, President Galtieri or whomever.)

"I feel very lonely without a war. Do you feel that way?"
--Winston Churchill to his doctor, June, 1945

Why do the older ones send the boys, their sons, to war?
The civil elders clash with clean words, far from fields of gore,
But each boy, oozing blood, becomes the statesman's whore.
Time was when kings of old would test and try their mettle,
Quick to the flashing steel, thick in the heat of battle,
Steeped in the fray till they won, or were vanquished by death's rattle.
What have the boys to do with their aging sires' struggles?
The boys with their lusty loins for loving and hugging and huddles?
The boys with their hearts in their eyes and their spirits afloat like
bubbles?
Let the boys sow their fields with loving, I say, and come slowly to
their future;
Let the boys reap life's sorrow slowly and come fully to their nature;
If the fading statesmen-and-women choose, let them fight and prove
their stature!
Let those who would fight go to battle, and leave at home the lovers;
Let those who seek might and power, fame, courage and pride join the
others;
While I, I'll stay home with the boys, and join them under the covers.

61

Voices in the Wind—A South African Ballad

When she listened with some care she heard voices in the wind,
And they swept around her ear lobes and etched pictures in her mind;
But the voices weren't new, she had heard them once before
When the voices turned to angry knockings at her kitchen door.
It was food that they had wanted, they would not leave her alone,
And they hammered and they clamored for a morsel, crumb or bone;
But they stepped beyond their bounds when they came so near her
home
And the fear clutched at her throat, but its force ran through her arm
When she lifted up a carving knife to keep herself from harm
And she swung it in the air, swung and lunged and plunged it where
An emaciated body housed the blade within its belly—
Strange to enter thus a body: strange food flashing, slashing, slushing
While the blood engulfed her doorway like a reddened geyser
gushing.
They took the mournful heap away: a girl of seventeen with child;
(The coroner said the kitchen knife had pierced right through the baby's
head.)
But she, she had her doorway cleansed, replaced the knife with one
brand new,
Hosted guests in gracious style who saw but the front door they entered
through;
While at the kitchen's no one came, no bulging bellies, no eyes with
blame
Disturbed her threshold, her silent days, her graceful peace, her
appeased flame.
But sometimes when the wind was high, when it came from out the
north or west,
It brought those voices back again, which pierced right through her
peaceful rest;
And the pictures flashed before her; eyes and bellies on a screen--

Bulging eyes, beseeching, begging, and the girl of seventeen
With the body she had broken, and the blood that she had opened,
But most of all her own fierce arm with its naked blade extended.
Yes, most of all her raging arm, plunging, its uncloaked hatred gap-
ing—The picture worse by far than all: her own fierce, lustful raping.

Emöke

Every Tree is the Forest

Emöke Zsuzsanna B'Rácz was born a sword in hand and a song on her lips...so every line in her poems has an edge, she has been told. Coming from an oppressed society but a creative and nurturing family she has come to write what she knows. "Every little thing that is saved is saved by love." She is a founding member of Burning Bush Press of Asheville, One Page Press, Hun-tees, Asheville Poetry Review, Women on Words and is the official translator of Katalin Ladik, a contemporary

and premier poet of Hungary. Published on both sides of the Atlantic (*New York Quarterly, Magyar Naplo, New Native Press, Nexus, Webster Review, Rivendell, Asheville Poetry Review, Women's Words, International Poetry Review, NC Literary Journal* and *Wordimage*) Emöke has been making words available to the world since 1982 at Malaprop's Bookstore/Cafe and Downtown Books and News in Asheville NC.

after e.e. cummings

The heaven I seek is in my mother's arms
The illumination I receive is from my father's dream
Words come as frequently as I whisper their names
Margit Ilona and Istvan

Women on Words

Books upon books
red bricks
blue sky
eight women
sharing
bending the world
with their words
Barbara wants everything
Sharlyn is deciding to
come back or not
Genie, Maria, Joy, Rachel, Nancy and I
practice the art
listening
Red bricks
black coffee
books upon books
Women on Words

eb minor

the birds call upon
april winds
under wings
over golden apples
it is your scent
that delicious golden
body over mine

or

the birds call upon
april winds under
wings over apples
it is your scent
the body over mine

Birdsong

Eastern Towhee
cardinal and the House Wren
morning coffee in bed
this is the morning the
doves that coo to each other
by our window,
sing the first sound of spring, I with them

still the sky
blueness foretells
the cold is still to come
ear drums flutter
spring and gale force winds
I fly on wings to you

now and always
you, just you

Amy Bloom at Malaprop's

She blooms every morning
she is tall, lips and eyes to notice
her voice surprises all who listen.

She likes mostly writers named Alice
prefers to read authors already dead
no extra words skirt her courtyard
her smile is forever there.

Poetry is her lover
the wind lifts her Pegasus
three kids kindle
fire and ice around her.

In a small town of six hundred
she lives near the post office
and a Dunkin D shop.

She wishes for a pad in Brooklyn
just for herself
and her Muse.

Hearth Mother

the sun
followed you
today
in your steps through the glass door
in this springlike March 15th
blind
force took your steps
above clouds
March will never be the same
Heat wave, frozen
dew covers the neighborhood
March winds above hearth
I am keeper
of memories of you
for you, Mother
of Independence, of interdependence
Mother of Holy Words and dreams
your kindness embraces
magical energy
no one can stop as it flows through
veins of this land
pouring, shedding yet
growing green buds of effortless
happiness just for you, the land

ss america

April 2nd 1964, Le Havre France
The train ride from Paris to Le Havre was
                    unmemorable.
The expectations of the ocean crossing were
                    enormous.
The expectations of seeing my father after eight years of separation
                    un-describable.
SS America was the name of the oceanliner
we were embarking on to arrive in
New York City, America
leaving Budapest and grandparents behind.
I had never seen the ocean before.
I had never even seen a large body of water
except Lake Balaton
which we called our "ocean"
in a country the size of Indiana.
The boarding for the oceanliner
was chaotic.
The photographer caught our picture
like frightened birds.
The steps down to our miniscule cabin
suffocating.
The window to the outside was
round and small.
Mother tried to keep us close at all times
but my sister and I were ready
to explore
off we went
without words we expressed to each other
the sightings of everything unfamilar
holding our breath and each other's hands
the harbor still within reach.
In the middle of the night
the oceanliner left Le Havre

leaving all we knew behind.
Before breakfast
we walked out to see the sea
holding each other's hands
forever
breathtaking
limitless
endless
blue grey
windworn
frightening
paralyzing
speechless we stood by the railing
holding our breath and each oher's hands
Leaving Budapest and grandparents behind
silence in our hearts
endlessly
the sound of the waves
reached and sealed a knowing—
no turning back!

Remember Fish

Remember fish
She whispered from a distance
The currents border-less
Smoothness and light
The dark through
Immense and everlasting
Waves
Meditate
Grateful

True Loves

four fifty-six a.m., Wednesday
the weather beckons me to wakefulness
the rain patterns my thoughts
the silence of a snowflake comes to mind
you turn and rest your arm where I am still warmest
it is the last cold breath of winter battling the sky,
snug and secure
in bed I linger to escape from my dream world
the hassles slowly take their seat
the shower matches the rainfall
I disappear in the music of water refreshing
day after day the soul that resides within
I think of my sister and brother, missing
their embraces and time for drawing at the dining room table
the colors jump from his to hers and mine
calling on different worlds that unite us yet each of their own
the distance feels like a separation
but in reality we reside close to heart...
no need to miss each other
true love leaves no room for lacking

Bernadette Bori (1976-2011)

it was the season of the hearts
when I heard you were ill
I felt immediately scared

me
being without your laughter
and the inquisitive looks

you
always bringing your questions

"where did I do that
how did I get that done
why did I not say things that needed to be said?"

you
calling on my responsibilities
without which
I would not learn my lessons

you
made me know you in an instant

you said the same
to your mother in explaining our connection
third cousin on my mother's side

you made us connect
you made me laugh
you made me cry

you
a spirited cry for justice

you
beautiful and trusting.

Harlequins

Your
Wanting victory
Urges the waves
Tomorrow is only an evening away
Serving lettuce to madhatter guests
Rabid thoughts and maddening depths
Peonies and ponies mixing the well of wishes true
Over the hills and borrowed moments
Neverland exists without us
Memories are the local guardians
Jokingly birds flit from branch to branch
Invoking silence
Harboring echoes
Gathering lightning
For winter is surely here
Every which way the wind blows
Deep Madness Drives nails into
Creases in the minds
Bringing whoever
Absolute nothing

Nothing absolute
Whoever Brings
The mind creases
Nails driven into madness deeply
The wind blows every which way
Surely winter is here
Lightening gathers
Echo harbors
Silence invokes
From branch to branch
Birds flit jokingly
The guardians and the local memories
Without those neverland exists

Borrowed moments walk over the hill
The well of wishes are true ponies and peonies
Maddening depths rabid thoughts
Madhatter guests serving lettuce
An evening away is tomorrow
Urging waves and want victory
Yours to be, yours.

In short
To be yours, yours to be
Deep madness driven and nailed
Tomorrow echoes the silence of the madhatter party
I am in neverland without us and invoking the queen
To bring ponies and peonies to words I lack

Forced Labor-Death Camp Recsk
spring of 1950 to fall of 1953

In silence, his thoughts and memories remain
No, I do not want to talk about that time
Like a mantra
With alcohol breath, hollow eyes
he repeats under his breath
I do not want to talk about that time
and denies himself release,
Fragmented life
imprisoned for life
800 of them.

Father, like a sleeping volcano
with memories of torture that
vibrated in every bone and the flesh.
He does not cry out now or then.

The stories of good deeds
Come like bullets when they are gathering
Survivors from the labor-death camp
… and try not to talk about that time,
But never is it without the shards embedded...

"Remember how B'Rácz called the guards'
Attention on himself…time and time again?"

He knew his limits and did his most
To careen the pain and punishment
Away from his frail and sick friends
Serving for no reason, without judgement
In this forced labor-death camp called Recsk.

Kistarcsa, Recsk or Siberia
The Gulags sapped young men
Of strength and vitality

Sickness, nightmares and physical abuse
Remained to remind them of the era
We do not talk about
We do not know about
We can not imagine why, how

Nations punished those who stood against the tide
Crimson, black, bile green souls
Enjoyed their power with guns at their side
The guards walked around like ghouls
Sowing fear …here take that, and that.
No food for a week
Stand in water

Naked in frigid December
Tied hands behind your backs, shackled
Now take that.
Another month in solitary
Again and again,
His cries remained silent and self-imposed.

Basalt mine, cracked hands, axes flying
Bodies falling out of line
He picked them up daily and carried them
Back to their bunk bed, gave them his food
Acted up to direct the punishment on himself
Endlessly
The whip came down on his shoulders
That held his son gently….years later
The sun burned their backs
Mining basalt in the quarry
Everyday for three and a half years

The poems written by Faludy were
Committed to memory by Nyeste
When needed to be written down
In their blood, no ink to be had
Toilet paper needed to be stolen, he stole it
Got a week outside in a ditch
The capillaries in his ankles died
Years went by and seven amputations later
He died. He took the bad breath of an era with him
Without spreading it onto his children
Silently he went
Even then.

There was only one time father opened up
Only once the alcohol loosened his lips
They beat me so bad that
.....I did not know if I was a boy or a girl...
That's all he ever said to me
.....I did not know if I was a boy or a girl...
And he laughed a short breath
That was under the Parliament before they took me
To the forced labor-death camp.

To give his youth for Democracy
Is what was called for and was taken.
Fear for lack of power ruled the time and the land
The villagers nearby knew and looked the other way
And even today the smell of shame lurks in their hearts
Even today, the ghosts of Recsk haunt the hillsides.

A National Park now, commemorating 800 lives given
Destroyed for a moment of indecision by a government
School children pile out of buses and can not imagine
What was given for their freedom in Recsk.

Andrassy Ut 60 was the beginning torture chamber
That now is a museum in Budapest called the Terror Haz.
My mother and I went, stood in line for hours three times
We entered and faced oil snaking around a tank, black mirror
Reflecting all the mesmerized faces
And the room where they hung them upside down from a hook in
The ceiling is intact, beating them with water hoses full blast
Pulling the nails off their fingers and toes
The hot iron that was used for prodding
All displayed as if still in use for
Branding animals…their cries were still in the air
My mother and I ran out of the room breathless
Knowing what went on in there, brought it to life with such force
For both of us 40 years later
The solitary tomb was no bigger than a cave for a midget
The father that came out of there was a ghost of himself
He shielded his children from the pain and suffering he knew well
The toys and the bread on the table every day
We could not imagine
We did not know this man's past
And understood less what sent him into fury
In our childish ways we expected everything
Brightness, happiness, good health for the man we held as our father.
The time was cut short for us to get to know
What was and remains buried in the past
Buried, but there too the guard on duty,
Armed and ready
To shoot at a whim, at any movement,
Fragmented life, like the quarry they worked, rocks
Frozen in time, gray and cold to the touch
His life held in prison
Even when the era was gone

We can not imagine
We will not understand...ever

We do not talk about
We do not know about

We can not imagine
Man's inhumanity to man.

Commandment

To live a life unselfish
Commands a Buddha on a Chinese fortune cookie
I look outside
I turn my head up
I see clouds against blue
The whiteness blinding
The sky embracing all shapes and intensities,
The speed matters to the sky not
I am from below gaping at the vision and the play
Of enormous physical bodies in the
Even more enormous universe that I am a speck of.

Selfishness is an art if done well and for the right reason
The Buddha says that happiness is my life's purpose and yours
That excludes selfishness, I understand that
And the practice of that is the challenge each day
Each day over and over again
Happiness.

Happiness
Each day over and over again
The practice of that is the challenge each day
That excludes selfishness, I understand that
The Buddha says that happiness is my life's purpose and yours
Selfishness is an art if done well and for the right reason.

Live a life unselfish
Commands the Buddha.

May 7,
Plant a tree for Rabindranath Tagore.

If you asked me today
what kind of a tree to plant for me
I would say a Linden Tree
the scent and the flight of the seedpods
the tree not far from our farm.

I am filled with a memory of Tagore's tree
I saw as a child of ten in Balatonfured
on a school field trip.

Tagore rested in the Heart Hospital there after his
European tour of 1926 exhausted him.
In thanks to the people of Balatonfured
Tagore planted a Linden Tree.

I remembered with surprise
that I chose the same kind of tree
that Tagore planted
which is of no consequence to
anyone but me, a Tagore fan.

I planted a Holly for my father
as my mother requested

I planted a ginko tree for my mother
as she collected ginko leaves
on Wall Street in Asheville
she had never seen
such bright yellow heart shaped leaves.

The Tisza tree from Transylvania
stands as a carved headstone in my backyard
symbols my sister and I scribed
into it to remind us of love

family and the short stretch
the visiting hordes are on this planet.

Plant a Tree anywhere you like.

Remembering our Aunt Julia
part one

My aunt Julia was the mapmaker in the family
Cartographer
in other circles.

She walked in heavy work boots across the land
Cigarette hanging on her lips
bent under the wind and her mother's scorn.

She idolized her older brother, my father
Followed him with hazel eyes in darksun brown skin
that held her rage, quite unnoticed.

Her words were always kind to us, the children
Warm hands on our foreheads
smoothed out our fears eased us to dream.

French words English words or Hungarian
She spoke and read while the ducks and geese had to be fed
each night dinner on the table by eight pm

She loved reading almost more than breathing.
Birthed two girls, lost one within ten days
Morning Glory grew strong by her mother's side
Each breath strengthened her child
for the world that is a struggle
to get a step ahead instead of sideways.

Can you tell which way she went?
I look in my heart to find the path
My aunt Julia scribed there.

Living

Without wings we fly
Learning
Windows
Open or closed

Reading of books, dancing
Opening
Blossoming
Again and again.

Open or closed
Closing
Opening
The act of searching

In attics and books
The possibility of learning
Here
There

Everywhere.

It is mid February

December tenth the
last time we did duets
I left town for six weeks and since then
duets have not crossed your
what we call this or that
may or may not last
yet I sing the song you
invite the harmony

the trees hear me laugh
the squirrel just hangs
the bird feeder spins

nice afternoon duet
of bird and squirrel
as snowflakes spin and flutter

the winter is not over yet
the sun is powerless even at noon
I feel only the cold of the wind
as it wraps around Walnut
to Haywood Street

Genie

For now, a focus on small things

In my writing, places are as important as characters, and the same holds true in my life. If the place is wrong I'll move on, and have relocated to more towns than I care to admit. Raised in Texas and New Mexico, I  migrated to Kentucky, New York, Pennsylvania and Georgia, before finding poetry and purpose here in the mountains of Western North Carolina. Poetry allows me to explore my observations, and if I can find the words to match the experience—I've had a good day. Some of these poems have appeared in "Western North Carolina Woman," "Rapid River" and "Does it Grow Corn."

West Texas

A children's sandbox
gone to weed at the foot of a torn
movie screen claimed long ago
by prairie winds.
From the playground
rows of speaker poles radiate
like pleats in a cheerleader's skirt.

In the Road

So many roads taken,
so many warning signs
dotting the shoulders.

And I've loved those warnings—
the negatives, the safety.
I've said no so many times
over so many years
to so many.

But now you.
Totally without warning,
there you stand.
And I cannot say no to you.
I cannot say no to loving you.

to l.w.

I taste a poem so fine;
the sweet words of another's
hand burrow deep
dislodging an ancient dream—
which floats now
in pieces
through my blood.

Composition

You favor jazz, crave it daily.
But you, my dear, are cello, violin and harp –
strings vibrating deeply, eternally.
You are not drums, not sax, not trombone,
not a single hint of jazz. I regret to
tell you this.

No, your notes are lyrical and impassioned,
your movements heroic and triumphant.
You are pure romanticism, my dear.
Beethoven's Ninth, perhaps,
but not jazz. Sorry.

Reflection

Today an odd thing:
I paused to listen
and not judge,
I paused to love
and not retreat,
and it was, oddly,
enough.

11:00 p.m.

From the night heat
an odd timpani,
as crisp June bugs
ping my bedroom window
like slow popped corn.

To a NYC Cop

You held a teenage girl
in your arms as she bled out
onto the sidewalk.
For years thereafter
you'd remember her hand
falling from yours
and you would sob.

But twenty years
have now passed, and
I wonder if you've healed
from her brown eyes,
from your promise to save her.
Or do you, even now, go to bars
and tell your story.

Shift

Too often my landscape
is poor and arid
stretching into eternity.
But now and then
a whiff of history,
or a small breath of truth,
winds slowly
around a corner.

Sweet Corn

Sitting in her wingback chair, Miss Amy
would eat her corn in the parlor. Of an evening
she could finish six or more.

Taking a steaming ear from the bucket to her right,
she'd pass it several times through her mouth—
her scattered teeth removing what they could.
She'd then toss the ruined ear into the empty bucket
to her left—even as she reached down for a fresh one.
Chewed kernels gathered in the folds of her green shawl.

Above her white head hung a forgotten quilt frame
secured by ropes and spider webs to the ceiling.
When the corn was gone, she'd sigh, rise slowly from
the wingback, and carry the buckets to the kitchen.

Petrichor*

I could smell myself.
My neck burned from the heat and I groaned.
Jerome looked over at me, the broom slowing
in his big hands. Jerome knew me, he did,
but he knew not to speak.

But Old Lev knew me, too. He paused his scissors
and turned his grizzled face at me.
He ran a quiet shop—dead quiet—the customer
in the chair was dozing.
"Careful, Boy-o!" Lev spat, "I'll replace you by
closing if I have to!"

Just then a wind, wet and cool, blew through the open door.
I turned and the rag fell from my fingers, sending
a wad of brown wax onto the pant leg of my customer.
The wax was barely visible on his black slacks.
I looked quickly at Lev, but his back was to me. Taking
two brushes to my man's boot I buffed until it fell to
the stand. He shifted, and I wondered if he'd seen.

I glanced again at Lev, who was rubbing his sciatic thigh.
Through the door I could see a dead workhorse, dry as jerky,
being dragged onto a low cart. How any city animals
survived this drought I did not know.

I'd just finished my man's boots when a second wind blew in,
followed by a thunder clap. Lev's customer opened his eyes and
Jerome looked to the door, his gray head rivered in sweat.
Suddenly there was joy and laughter in the room as the customers bet
on the possibility of rain. My man stood to go.

"Great job," he said, handing me four bits.
"But…"

104

"Keep it," he said as I stared at the coins in my
hand.
"Yes sir, thank you!"

He walked to the threshold, looked at the dark clouds gathering above
him and ran toward Ninth Ave.   And then it came, the rain, and as it
fell dust rose from the street and entered the shop.   And the smell of
it—the dust and the rain together—gave me joy, and I whooped.

"Damn you, boy…!" Lev began, but I was on my feet and
headed to the door.   I stood at the threshold, grinning as
a heavy rain pounded my city.   I turned to see Lev's squat figure
just behind me.

"I see…" he muttered, "…looks like we are finished for today!"
He hobbled to the sink and I rushed to the shine stand for my things.

"…but come all the earlier tomorrow, do you hear…?" he growled as
I ran into the rain.   "I'll teach you something—how to lather a man's
beard—do you hear me, boy!!"

"Yes, Sir!" I called over my shoulder.

petrichor – the smell of rain on dry ground.

Santa Fe Trail

A lightning flash
silhouettes a coyote
streaking four-legged
past scrub cactus,
past my window.

I would sooner join him
in the heat of the gathering storm
than sit another hour in this
cold Greyhound headed west.

Riddle

Knock, knock …
"Hello, my car just died.."
I plead to an old woman
peering though her screen door.
"Never have sons," she replies.

Blue Mountain

And then there were the early
morning moments, when the fog
curling off her slopes
would wet my cheeks
and freeze my thoughts.

And in those moments
I did know her—
when her breath chilled my eyes
and entered my mouth.

My Own Backyard

I have lived a frugal and wage-driven life.
I am vital still, but these days
more thoughtful and deliberate.
And it seems, at last,
that it has come to this –
a log cabin and a tiny apple
orchard in a mountain hollow.
I do not eat the apples, no.
I hit them with a baseball bat,
lofting them into the meadow below.
Hundreds of apples sailing
over an imagined ball field,
and that is joy.

I am without television, and take
mountain walks instead of turning
on the nightly news.
For now, I avoid stories of
politics and mayhem.
For now, a focus on small things.

It's early evening, and a young turkey
stands alone on a country road.
Unguarded, quiet as a shadow,
she cares not at all that
I am close by. Her attention is on
the pasture to her left –
to thick bushes of thistle and
pampas. So strange to see
a juvenile without a flock,
going it alone. Not one thing
can I do for her. Her black eyes
catch the setting sun.

Starting back, I pick a rock
from the road.
Purple and warm,
it nestles in my palm, comforts me.
And what is your history, ancient
stone? To me, in this moment,
you are as much a miracle as
all the rest.

Hooholler Cove

6:00 a.m.

She lists to the right,
my old cabin, her timbers
leaning toward sunrise.

Noon

Cow tracks in the snow
cover the skid
where we left the road.

6:00 p.m.

Deep winter white-out:
one fly and I, together,
glad to be inside.

Devil Fog

It began, they say,
by shearing off the mountaintop,
then fell in layers down
warm slopes until it reached
the village
resting in shadows below.

The cloud then crept
red brick streets and slipped
quietly 'round dark stores
and houses, until the sleepy
buildings were chained
in cords of gray.

Finally, they say,
the old church took notice
and thrust its steeple
through the cloud lying
heavy on the town—
and the fog, thus cut,
retreated.

Room to Room

My old lady walks the nights away
chuntering to herself as she treads the
worn floorboards of our paint-deprived Victorian.
I gaze out at the dark mountains and listen.

Over and again I hear her stop mid-step,
only to sputter and cackle, then continue on.
From the bed I'll ponder these laughing fits
but know I'll never have an answer.

At first light she drifts to the kitchen,
silently whips up a mean breakfast for us,
then flumps into an old rocker and fishes a
crossword puzzle from her knitting bag.

She'll pencil in a word—maybe two—
before her lids clamp shut, her jaw falls
open and I'll wonder, yet again, if she's
left me for a better place.

Lay Me Down

I did not, of course,
decide to be born or get to choose where.
And perhaps this early lack of choice
established a pattern of indecision for
my entire life – as decades of schools, jobs and
friends passed by without a word from me.

I trusted chance.
It guided me away from addicted parents and
into the lives of bolder, exciting people – including
one who sank his straw into my lifeblood.

Yet, here I am, somewhere in my sixties,
with real time to choose, if not the location
of my death, the location of my after-death.
And I have given this choice
some actual thought …

So, if you will, lay me down
in the hot seabed of the Texas Panhandle,
where I may mingle with the prairie grass and
the remaining shards of my father and my uncle:
Texas boys, loving brothers, hard drinking writers,
terrible fathers.

Yes, please plant me beside
my father and my uncle, under scrub
cactus and mesquite, and return me to the place
where I first knew something.

In Time

I saw a portal, closing.
I had no time to enter it myself,
so tossed in only my name.

Maryann

...turns inside the weight of change.

Maryann Jennings, unrepentant idealist and retired English teacher,

 misses being in the classroom with her students in Springfield, MA. An aging athlete, she relishes playing around with words, dancing, scuba diving, cooking, reading, fighting injustice and disputing immoral, capitalist oligarchs. "Song of the Heart Stick" won First Prize in the "Joy" themed 2009 Paradise Poetry competition in Northampton, MA and was published in the anthology *Hear a Poet, There a Poet*, edited by writer Leslea Newman.

Con Brio

Before the threshold of the dawn
    one bird in the black volunteers,
        its clear note declaiming

a deliberate solo in the east cornfield
    out with the sleeping turkeys
        then, dark silence again, still.

Dulcet scattered heartbeats measure and yawn,
    eyes seek outlines in slim light;
        the lone bird repeats the invitation.

Subaudibles percolate in the neighborhood gloom,
    throats clear but hesitate until
        the felt urge pushing, pipes.

And there! a lyric answer flings up,
    bright coloraturas ring trill,
        and the waxing constellation echoes

bell tones volley in chimed conversation:
    I'm here! The cat in the dark house is loose!
        It's morning! New seeds are out at the white house!

Their singular overture to this sunrise
    spills through cemetery and garden
        as blush blue light smears night.

Forsythia for my Father

When, by the Ides of March,
rain brings the brighter day
by day sun pouring, pulling urge to bloom,
I miss him most.

The hole is deep and wide
with mixed-in loam and peat
soaked with water, ready
for the awkward young forsythia
all arms and legs
to root and bloom,
using season's heal and turn,
the promise to bear truth.

He is the early yellow blasts,
honest spray of shout;
life sure once more
against bare dirt of brown and branch,
when newborn greens begin again
nature offers chance:
I plant the matching green
in naming arc of memory.

Time Measure
(for Deirdre Scott)

The tree chunk leans in the Science Museum
a slice poised alone in the spotlight—
fifteen feet on the wide
of royal Sequoia, born of Oregon,
all glisten now hypoxy polish.

From its core eye infinitesimal
line after line after pale against dark
ripple out beyond arms' reach
to span ages from Jesus to plastic,
all scars of catastrophe and climate.

Blue pins by the dozen plot the story—
    numbers, Columbus, an alphabet,
    indoor plumbing, zippers,
    space flight and frisbees—
our time travel road map in wood.

If we turn to interpret our own badgings of growth,
our internal emblems of blemish and glad
we find evident witness inscribed:
layers alternate
burly thick or thread narrow
to mark heavy passings of pain
and sharp intensities of joy.

First our own pinpoint start
then the wide labored ring of our birth,
there a glad thin stripe learning laughter and toes,
this thick assassination band of divorce,
the sharp joy of sex,
and murky, wide numbings of death.

If we ring as we grow from our own noble core,
each felt event a tidewater mark,
growing by sorrows buffered by success,
and joys companioned by pain,
where on our map can we pinpoint
the when we are orphan, all alone?

To Love Boats

My father floated when he danced
at the Butterfly Ballroom where they met
and later, at weddings—
floor movement like boats buoying
they enfold moving upright,
embraced and suspended
a near hovering in air
my mother uplifted in arms,
the pair turn into swirls
smooth step slide hesitate
past the celebrant guests
with old joy remembered,
they rhythm above me
a rolling smile glide
my father held leading my mother
all aglow radiant
my father matching on earth
that sensation liquid
drawn always to water
held yet in felt float
held in grace
in the Spirit,
and sailing the buoyant.

Below the Swimming Lesson

In pine green lake at day camp
    painted turtles pinstriped yellow
    their skeptical triangle heads peek
    above bass inside the deep;

no one told me
water holds like humming
    envelope of moving tissue
    fairy light brush of liquid
    at the corner of the neck and armpit
a something under up:

    a sensed float at shin and throat
    elbows arms and belly held,
    reaching fingers feather
    no touch but water trust.

April Moment

A duck was on the walk,
I had to stop.
Standing, up to his ankles in the cold puddle,
a mallard too soon.
I never knew ducks had ankles.

His iridescent green head bent to beak a sip
then raise to the sky,
water dribbling back into swallow as ducks do pray,
with an ass-feather waggle,
pintails coiled like spitcurls.

Then a duck yawn stretch of reaching wing
flashed out downy feather under whites,
he plucks up an orange foot
to shake the water cold and shiver and the other.

Stopped
by the forfeiture of gifts:
    no swim
    no waddle
    no fly.

Just duck,
standing to drink and pray
in the refreezing April puddle.

The Deer

When they hung the deer in the garage
it was still animal.
Her dad and brother and Fred from up the street
humped the carcass in,
shoving woolplaid shoulders
in the huff and eddy of cold breaths,
they heaved the young body
till it hung in outstretched leap,
hindlegs high
from the silver pulley in the ceiling,
the crossed hooves distinct.

They turn their backs and go for a smoke.
The girl thumbs the doorlatch,
reaching in the gap of weekend guns and men;
the deer alone takes form before her.
In breathless narrow lean
she looks at transformation nearly done:

a belly gone agape, hollowed out
from bowel on to stiffened forelegs
straight and quiet she stands—
the marbled interior of white fascia, fat, and cartilage
melding with the purple muscle
she does not blink—
sprung ribs like ladder rungs,
curve the echo chamber slowly
where swelled the heart and lungs once
her breath mist faintly curling—
then the brindle coat, thick and safe,
imaginably warm in this cold garage...

until they return
to orchestrate the final changes
with sliver whippet blade skill
cut and start the skin split round each leg
and peel it off
becoming hide and heavy near the neck,
leaving meat behind.

She turns
inside the weight of change.

Girasole Call

Still and seemly, sunflowers
line the gaze of memory,
all stalky monsters
imperiously border the garden edges
with asters at their ankles.

They lean lanky into the ends of summer
above warm tomatoes sagging split upon the vine
smelling of green gone to dust in dry late August.

Heaving plates of seed wobble in breeze heat
lifting in blue ceiling currents
to drift yellow blurring on the grain
as their faces move to mark the sun
and follow its ancient arc across
from morning to the hilltowns west of here;
each fat flowerface looking
long in amber light and shadow,

and in the evening damp of ripened grapes
nod lost,
confused by moonlight.

Years to Wampum at Nauset Cove

Homely quahog – sweet cherrystone –
grown in the quiet brine of bottom:
its layers plum and sheen by degrees of moon pull
inside the oval fist of shell
round the blind pink morsel.

Tide wash weave and time ripple it
near the shallows,
the modest bivalve bared
to the clever grab of a stalking gull
who shrieks to sky, fling shell down:
to rock and shatter crack
then blurt the clam fresh trifle.

Desolate bits and chunks of shell now
float and roll the water
in the ebb they sink to tumble;
sand and water grind
that silk the armor edges soft
then furthermore to gloss:
the inner creamy flooding
its purple satin currency.

Intersection of October
at Lucy Vincent Beach

On the tossing midnight beach a mile along the mingle
between wave soar and runneling ebb and hiss
our dog, with lowered head, whines.

Just beyond, held in sand
scoured by harvest moon high-tide,
there humps a rounded heap of shadow huge.
Closer, still blue pile of sea turtle, dead:
a pale barnacled shell the length of a coffee table,
belly up.

Blown to land by verging winter wind
the limpid carcass arrived to meet us
with our champagne in jelly glasses
for a "50 & Fabulous" romantic birthday beachwalk.

Stepping in the shush and blow surround,
dog and we make solemn circle
in matchlight fluctuating with the moon,
haloed by the rotted fishy brine of death.

Afternoon in Yellow Poplars

Up in the stacked hills above the river
where the firebreak dirt road
becomes dim grassy dents among the poplars,
you shut off the engine of your demon-blue Camaro
and it sits, squatting and ungainly in the yellowed light
ticking.

I hold the paper bag of shells
and feel the bright excitement of your grandfather's shotgun
as you take it from the trunk.

Clutching bag and cradling gun, I watch you
cram an old cardboard box into the crotch of a slender birch
ten yards off in autumn glow

beside me, you take and crack it open,
stuff your hand in the bag like grabbing for warm peanuts
the time we watched the elephants dance,
slot two shells in and snap it shut.

I stand away, color hammering up my throat
quickening
and you aim, fingering the trigger—
that held moment,
my breath and holy blood beat—

then blast of kingdom come to yellow leaves
blows in the reverberating hills
the riddled box in shreds.

Second Mowing

Unkie's west hayfield looks about half mown
in the noon heat white haze.
Sean—the first nephew—barechested lean
sits hunched in the saddleform steel seat,
driving the dumb tractor—
a red faded family McCormick Farmall
a workhorse all gummy with gitgoing grease,
the axles and guts chug and belch.
Steering his line
he turns a slick torso, puts a hand to the seatback
to mark the path of cut grass flicked into rows
coming green from under machine blades and tines
a churning wake behind him.
Time moves and even
rows of dry tangled green going gold
become hayfeed nourishment in hot brief time.

Glazed looking over the workhorse wheels,
the duty bores him, he slinks into his slouch
dazing of cold swim, cold beer, cold nothing—
an imminent dead end of nothing going nowhere,
the haunting blank holds him and his friends
trapped with no imagination
in a ditch of minimum wage.

Turning forth, back and more through the heat
numb to the throaty echo off the field-edge oaks,
he cranks the next turn,
twisting out of himself into a clear moment—
        he sees his straight laid clean rows
        honest, well done—
and pleased to his center, he decides.
He wipes down his face with his sweaty t-shirt.

In this drone of late June he will cross times untold
the sloping twisted field
inside heat and tractor growl,
the green mown smell hovers the insect air diffused
as grasses stiffen and dry.

Seven Dogwoods
(for Bob & Susan Harper)

In the belly of a fine-legged doe
or a crow with solemn wings,
seeds came along Brushy Mountain,
crossing below Payne's Knob
to deposit at the reach
of Long Branch Road.

Land for a house and barn
cleared and level, opening to the sun,
their lifted hearts held light
until the smiling hill let go rocks
the size of cars and trucks to plunge
in sweeping plunder
leaving bent and splintered timber
all in eighty-four seconds.
How they sank inside.

Something must be said, though,
for perseverance
and blooming where you're planted.

At the foggy end of Long Branch now,
seven dogwood saplings stand
outside a picture window
and the lace blossoms glow
in morning silver drizzle.

Song of the Heart Stick
(for Cody)

dog dog i'm a dog
gold and open oh my golly
smiley wagger here inside
brush and thump lean on legs
snuffle poke the laundry
whiffle sniffer nose up up
on the window paste a noseprint
there beside a ladybug
wander lie in doorway sun
groan eyes close on carpet yummy
ah the drama sigh of loll and wait

dog dog i'm a dog
say out or walk to release me
outside outside leaping yippee
random frequent chance departures
expeditions explorations
oh the urgent investigations
for the Grail of my Heart's holy
always in the out there hiding

it's a stick oh yes this stick
sweet intriguing teasing smelly
tasty stick oh stick my now
yes got my stick here all my stick
carried shredded chewed and drooled
limp and lumpy bent and sodden
bring my prize oh rapture home

135

Pray
(for E. Doherty)

...the last day arrangement
will be a handmade intention,
a sloppy bouquet breathing greeneries and flowers—
variegated daisies and black-eyed susans
by splay orange day lilies and white goose-necked loosestrife
neighboring balloon flowers blue
and poked through with liatrus and lavendar yarrow—
all plopped then arranged in a number ten can
of Hunt's Angela Mia Crushed All-purpose Tomatoes;
nothing like the aloof rose demanding
or cloying declarations of carnation loss,
but a worthy burst life arrayed full
in its practical tin can.

Nancy

Little Poems

Originally from West Virginia, Nancy
Sanders lives in Asheville, North Caro-
lina. When she was a child she liked to
read and "make up" limericks. She has
taken a couple of poetry classes and at-
tended a poetry group in Chapel Hill.
She likes to write short humorous po-
ems and poetry inspired by nature.

139

One

Dark clouds floating overhead
Leaves blowing in the wind
Wild turkeys on the lawn
A snake swimming in the lake
Bullfrogs croaking in the pond

Two

Gray slivers intersect light
Shades of pale
Dappled circles outlined in black
Envelope the fallen leaves.
Now, serpentine figures
Appear
Black forms morphing
Into crimson ones.

Three

Waiting is a study in patience
The zen of ennui
60,50,40,30,20,10,9,8,7,6,5,4,3,2,1
At last the doors open and
The lecture begins. I ask
Why did I wait so long?
For this oration to begin
I go 60,50,40,30,20,10..................

Four

This dynamic wind tortures everyone
The precious warmth
Is weakened by the flow
That permeates our exposed skins
Draining the comfort gained from
Sunny skies overhead.

From a lofty surface
Candy violet is watching me
I feel its gaze
Sneaking a peek at timed intervals.

A burning sensation
At the back of my neck
Signals its presence
Its intent I know
And can only wait
To see what is the purpose
Of it.

Five

She asked the dark skinned man
Are you an illegal alien?
No, I haven't been to Mars
Then what is that red rock
you're carrying?
And what is the red dust
on your car?

Six

It takes many centuries
To reach its full height
The Sequoia a thing of might
Might start small
And then it's tall
After many years
Of starting to crawl
Can man leave well enough alone

Patricia

Life Richer than We Dreamed

Born in England, married into America, and now retired in Asheville, N.C., Patricia (Pat) Harvey has worked as librarian, anthropologist/teacher, editor and gardener. Loved poetry in school; only found, much later in life, the pleasure and self-discovery of creating a poem.

Appreciate

: to enjoy and esteem
: to raise the price or value of
: to be sensitively aware of

I more appreciate each day
as I slow down, can almost see
the finish line and slowly trace
its beckoning.

The shapeless blur of constant speed
gives way to sharp-edged clarity,
a vista with each feather, leaf
and mountain clear.

My bank accounts are smaller now,
each cent and dime a work of art
displaying sculpted heads and dates
pressed in its form.

My world is quieter, more calm,
without the unrelenting screech;
I've now discovered joy and peace
in buttons 'mute' and 'off'.

I'm welcoming again the sounds of bees,
of whispering pines and distant waves.
I almost hear the secret sound of
one hand clapping.

Why did I take so long to learn?
I always had this choice to see
and savor every leaf, each tree,
instead of rushing through the forests
of my life

No matter; here I am, with time
and heart, however frail, to thank
the ghosts of years behind, and turn
to greet today.

Musing

I call my bossy muse Gardenia—she's not
a licensed classic muse (nor I a noted poet).
Sometimes she comes indoors, but much prefers
to catch me humbled on my knees outside
with dirty hands and endless weeds to fight,
a captive student, undeserving of
her brilliant wit, her deep philosophies,
but now and then responsive to her gifts.

    Some poems spring full-blown,
    complete and perfect: orchids
    impeccable and stately, admired
    throughout their long display.

    Some creep, uncertain, frail
    and scribbling on the earthy page:
    periwinkles fearful of the sun,
    not knowing if they're beautiful.

    Some push themselves into the show:
    laughing, bold and bawdy morning glories;
    seriously pugnacious: sunflowers,
    five feet high.

Gardenia loves them all. Today she's sitting
in the breezy shade, throwing fallen apples at my head.
The next one hits the right side of my brain
before I've chewed the one that's in my mouth—
such strange and tasty unrelated themes—
dead-heading flowers; my dying friend,
the dogs next door, my father's fishing boat.
The hail of apples overflows my pail
so then she summons up a thunderstorm
and sends me scurrying inside with this day's harvest,

to compose a lyric recipe, worthy of her gift.

I, Wave

I am!
  I race
    in ecstasy
      toward the shore,
        raising my unique beauty
          above all the lovely others.
          The sun admires, envies
            every sparkling aqua hue
              in my brilliant fluid perfection,
              crowned with regal foam
            that I throw, generously,
          into the applauding wind.
      There never was another just like me!

There never was but a brief bright tip
of the endless, timeless ocean.

Widowing

Born in thirties, I grew up among
regiments of relicts from World War One,
widows with songs to sing and tales to tell
to while away the days, the nights, the years.

Annie next door "Mrs. Watkins to you!"—
would push back her gray frizzy hair, touch my arm,
and intone her mantra, her poem, again:
"My Jack was such a handsome, clever boy,
he thought the world of me. He said my hair
was golden as the corn. He promised he'd
unbind my golden sheaf each day and kiss
my ears forever. We were married one
week before he went to war. He's buried
somewhere in France. We talk every night."

Bob Anderson came back a gasping man,
his lungs eroded by mustard gas,
his wife the target of his helpless rage
for many years until the day she woke,
chilled by the empty bed, the open door.
She called, she looked in all the rooms, and then
explored the garden till she saw the feet,
blue, bare and upright, as if surrendering
from the welcome grave of the rain barrel.
She pitied, griefless, then began her life.

An unwed widow was Miss Mary Grant,
'betrothed'—she used that word for life to James,
her fellow Oxford student, her one love,
who left his books, his cap and gown, his Mary,
to be an officer and end all wars.
In yet another war she was my stern
kind principal, preaching the horrors

156

of war, from the great battle of Thermopylae
to Agincourt and Waterloo, even
in the crowded shelter at our school,
as planes droned overhead and sirens mourned.

They're all gone now, and I myself am old.
For them, still young, there were no men to fill
the hollows in their lives: their empty wombs,
their unrequited dreams, their silent rooms.
And we, re-singled by divorce or death
and living long, must recreate, like them,
new lives, and make our peace with solitude.

Learning to Sail

A sailor's daughter always scans the sky,
lifts a wet finger to assess the wind,
breathes deep to smell the likelihood of rain
and never doubts which way is south, which home;
precisely navigating on her quest
the most intriguing isle, the sheltered port.

Sailboats make exciting, faithless lovers,
sleek and fast, inclined to sweep you off
your feet and slide you down the slanting deck,
then onward speed without a backward glance.

Wise to near-drowning, a sailor's daughter
stays alert for boomeranging booms
or sheets deployed to throw her overboard,
fully aware, prepared to swim alone.

Comfort Food

We called it her Cut-and-Come-Again cake.
She made it every week, enough for us
to take some back after we'd had our fill
each time we traveled home.

Her apple-mint jellies, perfect with lamb
and new potatoes, shone like emeralds
in the row of jars as the morning sun
caressed them on the kitchen window sill.

We always said she over-cooked the peas
and cabbage, freshly gathered from their beds;
the Yorkshire pudding just a bit too brown.
Yet each familiar meal was heavenly.

When she was found, grounded at ninety-five
that day in June, a lamb chop, defrosted,
was waiting to become her Sunday lunch,
with clotted cream and berries for dessert.

Her flavors linger in our mouths, our hearts.
We never found her recipes.

Late Shift

Three fifteen a.m. The mockingbird practices his aria,
each trill, already perfect, repeated anyway
just for the joy of it, no competition at this empty hour.
I am a grateful audience of one, delighted to be once more
given this season of open-windowed nights.
The adolescent moon has set behind the mountains,
leaving just enough glow to silhouette the great oak,
newly dense with green, this clear May morning.

The steady purr of distant highway traffic
reminds me that the bird and I are not alone;
there's diverse wakeful company this godly hour:
truckers, adulterers, nurses, jazz musicians;
weary hotel workers going home; passionate bakers
heading to their yeasty ovens; the young woman,
contractions every two minutes, speeding to the hospital.

I used to fret at this unbidden wakefulness,
afraid I'd crash before I could afford to,
in my regulated days of stern responsibilities.
Now I am old and free to shape my hours
to my own whims and needs, to seize the days
or nights for whatever gifts or challenges
they throw my way.

Tonight, at four fifteen, silently, gratefully,
I sing with the wakening bird
then turn off the light and listen,
deeply, in the dark.

Golden Anniversary

I guess it's still an anniversary,
exactly fifty years since we were wed
with heartfelt promises 'till death do part'
that echoed in that huge old chilly church.

For many years, it seemed, our life was charmed,
endowed with earned degrees, a lovely child,
and grander houses every time we moved
on up the ladder. Earnestly we swore

there was no gap, no continental drift,
until we could not hear each other's rails,
although we shouted loud and louder still.
So, disobeying vows, I sailed alone

towards a life of freedom to explore
strange worlds, and to discover my own self.
The journeys, and the ports, have taught me well.
And now, surprise, we are each other's friend,

we meet from time to time and tell our tales
of very different fantasies and trails.
Tonight we sit and raise our glasses high
to celebrate lives richer than we dreamed.

To Love Like That

She was a good mother, everybody said,
and we knew that, too. Home late from the shop,
she cooked and cleaned, made sure we went to bed,
homework done, by nine. But she did not stop.

I never heard my mother talk of love.
She spoke of work, of family and pride;
told us strange tales of a town called Lvov
where she was a child, and so many died.

Now, side by side, my son and I, we sit
and as she talks, I hug him, stroke his cheek.
Her sudden tears surprise us all. "Regret,"
she says. "Times there, back then, were hard and bleak,
with six of you, needful, in our small flat.
I never had time to love you like that."

No Bother

The little smile, the softened brow,
your reading glasses low on your nose;
you looked so well-at-ease and,
at the same time, quite triumphant,
as you always did when you won at whist
or finished a crossword puzzle.

When we were kids your parting words
if we were off to someone else's house
were: "Don't you be a bother to them!"

At ninety-five, some twenty years of living
quietly alone, bothering no one, you were
severely bothered by a stroke. For weeks
you lingered, wordless but communicating,
helpless but in full control. You fretted
that you were a bother to we three
who gathered in; we owed you life itself.

When things seemed fairly stable, Rob
took family to Spain as they had planned.
Tony hurried west to check on things at home.
I stayed, and spent the usual two-to-five p.m.
reading to you, showing photographs of
the great-grandkids in Brisbane, and promised
to be back for seven-to-nine.

But I was called back earlier, to find that you
had slipped away, had made the necessary move
to win, to be no bother any more.

Lunar Elapse

Beaming and brash—the only one
  who visits now at night—the moon
    invades my room, opens my eyes,
      demanding that I wake.

      It follows as I shift across
        my bed, turn my back, refusing
          to admire again its fullness,
            its loony faithfulness.

          Old lunatic, I lie alive,
            content to forfeit sleep for one
              more menstrual reminder of
              my luck at being here
              and knowing that I am.

Something of Myself

My father wove fine fishnets by the fire
at night; caught lobster, herring, skate and
bits of sunken boats, and made me see
their beauty and utility of form.

He loved to sail his master's yacht, Hebe,
keel visible, sails slamming, reckless.
He battled wind and tide to win against
'the toffs' who sailed their own.

'The Jolly Sailor,' where he drank, played darts,
and told wild tales—all at once—was his home
away from home. I watched from the "Ladies's Room"
where wives and kids sipped lemonade.

He dreamt and talked forever of leaving,
of taking us all to Tasmania,
Vancouver, South Africa, where he could
"really make something of myself."

He died too soon, when I was twelve.
He left me his face, his skillful hands,
his wanderlust. His rage against the locks
of class restraining him.

I've visited the lands he longed to see,
and others too. I've grabbed the chance of
schooling he could not. I've followed my own
passions, dreams and paths and made my own
mistakes. I hope he would be happy, proud of
this 'myself' that I've become.

Waiting for High Tide

In nineteen eighty five I lived in sight
of Robben Island. My room faced westward
over Cape Town's bay to where Mandela
still was held, silent and solitary,
biding his time until the day when change,
implacable, set him free to lead
his people and his country toward hope.

On shore the tide was beginning to rise.
In genteel Grahamstown buses were burned
on highways in the black (un)settlements and
white scholars at Rhodes cheered the black cause,
reached out across crumbling barricades.

In Jo'burg wealthy whites secured their lives
behind electric fences, soaring walls
and guard dogs trained to smell out lurking blacks.
Many who ventured out to risk for change
happened to fall to their death from prison windows.

In Cape Town center Black Sash matrons—white,
impeccably dressed, mute—day after day
stood, flinching but unmoved, as men in cars
drove by and spat on them and their placards
that urged justice for all South Africans.

In Parliament since nineteen fifty-three
Helen Suzman—the only Prog, a Jew,
the only woman—argued at every session
against Apartheid's vicious, greedy laws,
never winning, never stepping back.

The famous Dutch Reformed Church dominee,
Beyers Naude, at last released from years

of house arrest, again cried "Shame! Repent!
We must make a joining trek this time"
to all his fellow Boers who'd kept the faith
in apartheid and bloody dominance.

In nineteen eighty nine the flood surged high
and swept out the old regime; Mandela,
ashore and free to lead toward the dream.
From half a world away I continue
to watch, hoping the tide will lift all boats.

Varanasi

As I sat, semi-comatose, addressing endless envelopes
a friend walked in and, wordless, dropped a face
on top of John and Irma Blakely, South Street, Waterville.
The photo, 4 by 6, filled all the room, inhaled its air.
The piercing eyes—red-laced, uncompromising, calm—
shocked me awake and hurtling back ten years
to my last Varanasi pilgrimage.

At dawn the *sadhus*, wandering monks (perhaps this very man was
there), already bathed and chanted on the *ghats*, the Ganges water from
their pots bouncing low sunlight off their streaming bodies as it fell.
The boatman, Mun, was waiting for me at the usual spot. We headed
out against the flow. The yellow mansion of the harijan who made his
fortune at the Burning Ghat, slid by, stone elephants trumpeted triumph
from the roof. The richest Hindus come to die in Varanasi so that their
ashes go straight into the arms of Mother Ganga at this most sacred
spot, their spirits freed from the wheel of death, is handled only by
despised Untouchables, who charge the Brahmins well for fragrant oils
and sandalwood to mask the stench of flaming pyres all day, all night.

Northwest, at Rishikesh, another sacred place, the Ganga's pure and
clear, born daily from the snow of Himalayan peaks. Varanasi she
is stained and weary, slow and broad, and burdened by carcasses of
sundry lifeless sea-bound things. Some are more blessed than most,
they ride the incarnation wheel no more. The holy men and newborn
babes are pure enough; the lepers and the mad have paid their dues in
suffering this time around. These all, at death, swaddled and handed
to the river, flow to Nirvana without need of purifying fire. A *sadhu*
(could it have been this very man?) told me of this as I sat on the steps
one afternoon when James, on a dare, swam out for a full immersion
in Mother Ganga's balm, and came up gasping, shivering, and telling
me how he bumped into a bundle, a tiny hand beseeching him from the
tangled cloth.

That night we stood—five paler dots edging a sea of somber Hindu men—and watched the three pyres reaching high as sons and brothers circled, feeding oils into the greedy flames, intoning formal grief and last farewells. The nearest corpse, a woman shrouded red—the men are wrapped in white—had been escorted to her final bed an hour before. The flames had eaten first the shroud, red canceling red, and then the hair. Now flesh began to drop away and long bones slowly showed themselves, like darkroom negatives, against the radiant coals. Her bright teeth smiled, unfettered now from modest lips and social rules. We strangers had been noticed, and ignored, after we'd asked some nearby men (one like the one I now have here) if we might quietly observe their rites.

Next morning, gliding by the *ghat* with Mun, the early light caressed the shapes of boys, knee-deep where Ganga caught the ashes. They bent and dipped their baskets in the murk, sifting sand and seeking treasures; a nose ring or a golden tooth that they might trade for rupees or a meal.

Above them on the steps the *sadhu* stood and watched, still and perfect as a heron, waiting for my friend to bring his camera.

To Young Robin

My lying window offered you a forest,
a whole new shadowed space to claim, even
a new brother, rushing out to greet you, but
yours was the only neck to snap against the glass.

I heard the crack, saw you tumble, lie fluttering.
Your heart pulsed light against the palm
of my hand, your beak grasping last sips of air.

'Don't go,' I said, 'I'll hold you till you can fly again.'
'Don't go,' I said, even as my fingertip knew
the impossible bend of your neck.
No more heartbeat; beak still; grey wrinkled eyelids
slowly lowered. Only the wind moved your feathers.

My hand absorbed your warmth, my eyes
feasted on the complex beauty of your peach-speckled breast,
the elegant engineering of your legs, one claw now
curled tight around my little finger.

I spread a wing and gazed, rapt and timeless,
at the long grey-silver pinions that launched
your final—perhaps your first—and fatal
exhilaration of racing into unexamined air.

To me you brought surprising grief.
And gratitude.

Go Now

We knew this was a one-way path—
no point in yearning to go back—
yet much of our delight in these ten years
was in recall of pieces of our past,
of people, times and places we were given.

Your memory of then stayed clear and true,
still lit with laughter at the fun we'd had,
some tears for ancient sorrows, gratitude,
and courage on your final journey home.

As more of you retreated from this life,
we created offbeat ways, laughing loud
as we revised those necessary tasks
in the bedroom, bathroom, church and outside world.
And always we found comfort in God's hands.

Today, as you do softly disappear,
I thank our God and you for these last years,
the happiest, most intimate, we've shared.
Already I miss you. I kiss you, and
happily say, "I always will love you.
Go now to God."

Haiku

1.
Dawn. An old man walks
from hospice, bowed by the bag
of her things, his grief.

2.
March in Savannah.
Pale northern tourists stagger,
blinded by loud green.

3.
Elaine sits behind
the Times, her hair alive with
dying winter sun.

4.
Arthritic live oaks
raise tormented limbs and pray.
The sky is silent.

5.
Lying in bed, eyes
closed, hands on heart, rehearsing
for the coffin scene.

Autumn Beauty

I *almost* fall for those commercial lies—
on every screen and page—that, aging, I
am uglier each day; that I must lift
my face, smear my skin expensively to
"take off twenty years" of hard-earned lines,
contort myself according to the style
of nameless skinny plastic aliens.

I find this ancient tree so beautiful
that I am bound to stop, to gaze in awe.
Amber flaking bark holds the setting sun
like sparkling jewels, freely tossed at me.

Its massive surface roots, gnarled and weathered,
remind me of the back of my own hand,
the hills of jagged joints, the winding roads
of veins, the wrinkled face of autumn earth.

One broken limb points proudly at the clouds,
adorned in all of rainbow's shifting shades,
triumphant, as they roll toward the dark.
Dying leaves lie, perfect in their decay.

Behind it all the massive mountains curve,
infinitely older than all they behold,
recede their peaks in paling hues of blue
until they merge into the universe.

Grateful, pensive, I head for home.
I worship the beauty of age, of change
and impermanence in nature's rich realm,
admire the grace with which live things die.
How did we, the Elders, lose respect
for who we truly are?

Piri

Every Little Thing is Everything

Piroska B'Rácz Gibson was born in Budapest, Hungary. She and her sister Emöke nurture the love of family and the arts. She is like the beauty of the wind on a summer eve before the temperature drops into sleep. Reading, writing and drawing are also her constant companions.

175

reflecting

the room is full of
still blue waters
the ripples
i make
are my own
shining
reflecting thoughts
of the name
i was given
the rivers
the sky
the earth
in red

Remembering our Aunt Julia
part two

my aunt Julia's eyes
like melting lava
the warmth that made you feel so
you don't know
where you are but
in love where you are
no questions and
no answers
stay and relax
the world can wait
you are here
being loved
definitely

mother

i would have said to you
let me know what it is
like to be not
here anymore,
kisses and hugs
holding hands, tears
and knowing no
more time,
still there is
a special twinkle
in your eyes
spread across
the sky, says
learn
the meaning
of this life
your own,
and still
this baby was fed
by drops of
sweet milk
mixed with honey
and the nights
were endless
while i loved you
in my sleep

Sena

Dragons Know the Secret Places

Sena Rippel was born in Los Angeles, California. She has lived in the Northwest, Southwest and New England. For the past twelve years she has called Asheville, North Carolina home. Besides writing, Sena works in stained glass, collage, and paint. All of her art forms are flavored with the essence of the many places she has lived.

Hibiscus Man

I have returned
to whence I came
Today
Hibiscus Man

The honey touched my lips
Sweet
but stung sometimes
A burning hidden in your heart
punishing me for my transgressions
For not caring that I stole
from delicate Hibiscus women
nectar
which was not mine
Yet more precious
because I took so boldly
my sensual delights

I took the pain in stride
knowing that in time
it would vanish
Sensing I would retain
the passion of your liquid life
glistening in my veins

For I was species
freckled child
Stealing
not apples ripe for eating
but pollen for birthing

Stirred beyond stirring
Alive beyond living
Not of father
mother born
nor sister
brother
friend
I am child
Woman Glowing
Lover of Hibiscus Man

Mourning Has Broken

It is in morning I wait
As magenta rose and paling Prussian blue
streak the softness
to blinking out of stars

It is in mourning I wait
Waking from too much dreaming
Hoping to open my eyes inward
upon a cleanscape
illusioned only
in the colors of my choosing
Longing to sweep across heaven
with soul bared fibers
pulled all the way out
streaming
flashing
rolling in wisps
Ethereal
Floating across the pale man's face
behind mandala moon
Grasping at what falls from star bound flights
trailing wildfire before my eyes

It is in morning I wait
Slowly transitioned into mortality
clothed in dewy infant tones
assigned only to the innocent

When mourning
Morning is the time to dream

Fallen

I am the pain Queen
that was your gift to me
You've buried me in your life
Now you want to heal me

Only soaring Gods
restore the vanished
So take my wings
they are singed
and dirty things
drifting too close to the sun
dragged upon the earth
in all the rough places

Saints do not pursue Clinton Street
Walk with me there
side stepping sorrows
Let me sway by your side
to music dripping of better days
and I'll set you free
before your shadow leaves me

Just say the magic words
Give me something clean
Give me a heart
for this consecrated body

Tell me why I should go
back into the wilderness
or kiss the sky
that wraps its blues
around my shoulders
Or fall into the hollow sounds
our voices have become
Goodbye Mr. Somebody

Limbo

I love you
Do you know how much
Yet I am damned
before your heart opens
Hesitation
rips this childish heart
makes it bleed

I am compelled to touch
the turn of your arm
the curve of your chest
I want to capture
the scent of your breath
pull it deep inside

When you leave
I am afraid
always
It is the hesitation
the silence
the moment without words
without air
without hope

I am a waterfall full of you
I cannot pause

I am undone until you touch me

Transformed

Taking stock
Making changes
Letting go of this
Letting go of that
Disconnecting from the drama
of so many peoples' movies

Some do not understand
or approve
of this new person
Not knowing how to react
Not knowing they don't have to

Everything struggles to blossom
It is an imperative
within the heart
Roots become stronger
run deeper
All else awakening
Streaming
surging upward
bursting forth into authenticity

We know we are born
We know our bodies will pass
into a different kind of earth
It is the living in between that counts

Not always gaining
Not always losing
But finding the clarity of ourselves
in the balance

After Midnight

At night the moon draws wavering silhouettes on my wall
as I drift into that place where only children go

I come to consciousness knowing he is there
behind me
leaning in the doorway on his stick legs
He is watching me sleep
I know his silence

The Spongeman is patient
He will not wake me himself
but will wait in the darkness watching
The slightest movement will betray me
He wants to pretend I choose to offer myself up
a sacrifice

I lay frozen pretending I am invisible
I know I am food for him
If I move or make a sound he will absorb me
pulling the strands of my little life into himself

I am afraid
He visits now and then
when the world is wet and silent
He is not a dream

Sometimes he approaches a little closer
I can feel his breathing from deep within
A sucking that is almost soundless
He wants my innocence
my sweetness

This night will last for a very long time
If I am careful I will survive intact

When dawn approaches he will remove his gaze
Suddenly he will be gone
Then I can breathe
I will hold down the tears of relief
curling up from deep inside me

When I wake, I will dress, comb my hair
I will go to the table and eat my Cheerios
My brother will look at me across the table
I will know if the Spongeman visited him, too
I can tell because his eyes are vacant
We will not speak of the Spongeman
because it is unspeakable

We will go out and play war with my brothers' friends
They let me play because I am good at dying
I have had a lot of practice
I grab my heart and dramatically fall
rolling down the hill, arms flailing
I crumple at the bottom in an unnatural position
I do not breathe even when they try to revive me
I can hold my breath for hours

If I survive two more nights
I will be glad to go back to kindergarten

Grace

If I am wise
then wisdom lives in a place once carved out by pain
If I am strong
then strength is a hard earned shield
If I am kind
then I have walked mean and narrow streets
If I am bold
then I have been held back by misfortune's icy grip
If I have beautiful imaginings
then I have gone into that night where nothing breathes

I do not desire to sleep alone
Yet I am most brave
solo
inside my dreams
I am my hero in that place
between yesterday
today
and all of my tomorrows

Is there any action that is always humane
or hands that never hurt
Are there ever days when peace survives
vanishing not
with the crossing of the hours

I fear venturing out on immaculate sand
my footprints shining close behind
Yet I am drawn out
for the tendrils of me crave the moon

If I know what is sacred
then I have been defiled
If I am compassionate
then I have traveled the river of sorrow
If I am serene
then I have known chaos
and wandered in that ancient place
where Gods are always merciful
where breath is shared
and life is wrapped like a treasure

Maze of all I've known

I have to thank you for the inspiration
You have bled me all the way to poetry
Comfort with you I've never known
just burning without a prayer
Should I have known my antithema
how much you feared the changing
when you came wounding
staggering through my life
crashing into walls of my well being
You were a welcome burden
for a while too long
Should I be grateful for your failing,
falling, gnashing, collecting my blood
for unfortunate transfusions
You claim you never made your mark
yet your life is a legacy
etched into my flesh
Now all is quieting except the distant echoes
where pain is numbing sweetness
lingering in the aftermath of you

Everlasting

It is my birthday
Each morning as the sun rises
Each time my children draw breath
Each time my grandchildren giggle

It is a shining thing
to experience so many childhoods
so much life to dance around
so many smiles to revel in

What is age
but a passing of seasons
regulating the tides of being
Yet joy does not age
only increasing spirit
while the body mellows
Cycles of days and nights leave behind
visible remembrances on skin
wrinkles, scars, laugh lines
Proof of life

Today it is my birthday
Becoming always something new
Ageless

Pretty Baby

I sewed Dolly's arm back on
She smiled the whole time
not betraying so much as a twitch
I almost thought she enjoyed it
Maybe it made her feel human
to be torn asunder
then healed
Or did silly Dolly even know
Now I see Dolly's head is loose
bobbing left and right
stuffing showing at the seams
Yet Dolly is still grinning
Her eyes are twinkling
Should I feel sorry for poor Dolly
not aware that she's falling apart
or envy her

Still

There is a still sadness in my soul
that comes now and then
remaining till broken
as a pebble breaks
the still silence of a pool
I'd rather ripple my life outward
in a circle
yet the still sadness requires my attention
until the pebble flies

The Best

I hold out my arms
Jewels of myself
held in open hands
an offering to humanity
to help in the shining

Sometimes sorrow is received
Sometimes pain
Hardening these gems
Forging their brilliance
Making them more precious

It is in the giving
the best is received

Walking with Heaven

Walking with heaven above our heads
the faithful always suffer
brimstone lights our way
close to the earth

Flying words thrown
from a hard mouth
leaking truth
and other obvious things
Close to the earth

Our feet dancing wildly
Moving blistered limbs
Trying to soar cautiously upward
Close to the earth

Too too close
Close to the earth

Silence in Cocoon

Tears rolling down inside
merging droplets rivering
Centrifugal pain
dealing a hard invisible hand
Heart really breaking
I can hear it this time

Why does this smile arise
From where
Will I explode in silence
or merely leak

Dragons Know the Secret Places

I-She should have known
sometimes sensing is not enough
Hanging on
for inevitable glide off cliff

Woman
I say reflecting
thou hast reached the vanishing point
Cha!
I-She say Whoa
brakes me here
Peeling skin
burning memories on God only knows whose road
Ahh
I have understood enough
I have walked invisible trails
always lacking perfection
I-She is defectability
Seen?

Read me a story
Put flowers on my head
I-She gone mad
forward inching only
I did too much flying
I crawl now
watch toes disturb dust
meditate on prints left behind
Watch for lion

Prophets sing loud
they live it not
their dead
transcended into blunders

escaped into holiness
convenient is

Weak survive
Strong kill
Clear go crazy

I-She woman sees the future
can't tell though
crystal ball say secret
Big secret

Eclipsed can mean beautiful or gone
Dragons beyond this point are

Enduring

When I awake
my soul to flake
and pass away with dew
Always there are specters
always they are you

Virginia

Learning to See in the Dark

Virginia Haynes Redfield grew up in Miami, Florida but has lived happily in Asheville, N.C. for the last sixteen years. She appreciates greatly being part of the Malaprop's community. Her upcoming memoir is titled "Night Bloom: Learning to See in the Dark."

About Sex

It's like cantaloupe
Big luscious globes
Striated skin
Orange meat
Barely hidden by thin rind.

Take a spoon
Plough into a crescent firmly, gently,
Juices oozing from cut edges.

It's like angel hair
Thin strands of al dente pasta
Bathed in fruity light green
Olive oil, gently pressed from
Sun-baked olives.
Cloves of garlic,
Surrendering,
Float among the pungent bits
Of parsley and basil.

Separate the strands
Savor the aromas
Wish for a mouth big enough
To contain the whole.

On First Living Alone

I come home
not like a letter slipping into an envelop where it belongs,
but like a tourist in someone else's life.

"How nice everything looks.
Wonder who lives here."

I touch the dark wood of the round table,
take in the flow, flat-bottomed chair near the window,
waiting.

Silence except for the whirl of the refrigerator
and the soft flap of the paddle fan
hanging from the ceiling.

I turn on the standing lamp, though it's still light outside.

Zoe

...and I laugh in wonder at myself.

Zoe Harber recognized her call to publish her writing when she read a remarkable poem by a Vietnamese Buddhist monk, who is also a woman. Zoe attempts to speak with her readers about spiritual and psychological experience without imposing a point of view. She has formally studied world cultures and traveled extensively in both the east and the west. Formerly, she spent thirty years as a licensed psychotherapist specializing in working with children and their parents.

The Lady Shigura

At the moment of plucking her eyebrow
Lady Shigura attained the supreme awakening.

Her famed throat, delicate as a morning mist,
let escape a single syllable:
"Ah!"

The ladies in waiting sent word to the east guard.
Moments later, the chief administrator
firmly interrupted the dream of the Lord Shigura.

Footfalls like distant thunder
swept through the hallways leading to the western wing.
Lanterns of the children's quarters suddenly burst into light.

Unannounced, Lord Shigura thrust aside the panels to his wife's
chamber.
A slight moisture from his hand darkened the sheen of the thick rice
paper.

Lady Shigura was seated on a scarlet pillow.
When her husband had entered, she gently rose.

Her eyes sparkled like raindrops on a collection of diamonds.
With a cry of joy, Lord Shigura bowed.

Santa Maria de las Ramblas de Barcelona

You make a fool of yourself
waiting for me outside the house.
From my window
I pretend I don't see you
all dressed up in
your latest infatuation with yourself.
But you're out there, alright, not even getting off the Vespa,
straddling it, shorts so short they show your crotch,
shirt half knit/half buttoned
and you're gunning the engine like time
lasts only seconds before old age begins.
Eternity is just a cozy coffee break in your story.
Yet
you are always impatient for my love.
One would never know, other than myself,
that you
—impatient but refined
discreet, tastefully ardent—
are a most wonderful lover.

Were.
I hear you calling out—yelling—my name,
"our" name,
your pet name for me
that only we share.
You blast it to smithereens.
You're ruining things
by blabbing my name,
making it obvious that we are lovers,
showing off your body like a hooker.

Honking now, all hyped up,
waiting for me to fly through the smog to you,
wanting me to jump on, yelling

214

"take me anywhere, big guy. Into the blare, the glare, the leafy
boulevards,
anywhere you want, just take me, babe."

But I stand at my window watching from behind the curtain.

Now you're honking, gunning the engine, shouting.
What happened to the subtle stranger who
guided with exquisite care my liberation?
Who came to me at dawn two winters ago
tapping on my window,
quiet as leaves tumbling on snow,
taking my love in the alleyway as profoundly as
a great artist accepts a masterpiece entrusted to his passion?

I try to meditate.
Instead I hear your heat sear into my blood
as it always does when you long for me.
Except today I try to resist
'cause you're acting like I'm a drive-in dry cleaning specialist
who's upsetting you by taking too long.

Is it my blood that pushes me to fly to you?
Or that someone will, so it better be me?
Nobody else belongs on the back of that Vespa,
speeding through the so-called wind,
holding myself on fine
but putting my arms around your hunky body
as if I'm about to fall off.

Your chest holds me to you
through the back of your torn t-shirt.
From your chest comes energy that
pulls down my camisole,

so my boobs are warm and tight as I push against you
as we race through the streets
as the air becomes gently dark
and I'm so turned on I laugh with wonder at myself—
why did I hesitate?

Your friends are hanging out in a park, so we drop by.
I get off the bike,
let the guys get a good look at my ass,
then go over with the girls, smiling, while they check me out.
Tight jeans, tits half out of my shirt, make-up heavy and sexy—
I look like them and I'm feeling ok,
but then you tell them all my name—
our secret name;
they use it like Lucy's or Guadalupe's
while they talk to me about clothes
and it isn't special any more.

I stay with the girls.
Street lamps pool light on their heads.
I glance up and your eyes are swimming,
the pupils so wide in love you look drunk.
You are seeing my enlightenment
while I stand with the girls in my tight jeans,
light pooling on our heads like halos,
making us glisten.
And when I look at you feeling like that about me,
I finally know for sure—
it doesn't really matter what you call me.

In a Village Near Benares, India

He awakens with a falling sensation.
Snuggled next to him, overweight and snoring,
his wife lays sleeping.
He groans inside. Like a fool he's made her pregnant.

She slips her leg, still slender,
between his burly ones.
Her breasts push against his chest.
He remembers his first sight of her...
his bride-to-be – sixteen, she was,
ripe and full of love.

In her arms, Sanjay, their little son, is dry and peaceful.
Nearby, his desk. The bills are folded neatly.
Otherwise, their home, a single room,
is the usual mess.

He quietly sits up.
First light glides in on a shimmer of heat
the room turns peach, then abalone pink.
He should leave soon—but doesn't move.

The automatic "on" switch
of the battered electric coffee pot
clicks;
water drips...
and then that wonderful smell...
He doesn't even try to resist this
morning coffee with cream.
another wasteful western extravagance...

Mira shifts and softly kisses Sanjay.
From the temple comes
the drum's loud haunting drawn out thump!

the men—first one calls out then all begin
raggedly in unison they sing
the ancient names.

After so many years, the first cry sung still gives him chills.
He glances down.
Why won't Mira understand?
He could never like Bombay;
his life is here, since his birth, his childhood here and
now he is one of the men;
men who praise with sound and word
the treasures of five thousand years.
Today he stays in bed
letting sound wash over him.

Beloved music ends.
Full dawn makes fiery red the walls.
His soul returning to his skin…hesitates…
and in that space The Mystery reveals itself—
that it indwells in each cell
in every inch of his home this room
messy tiny ordinary.

He reaches out his arms to hold the three of them.
These are his jailers.
This is his prison.

Mako

She began her service as a lady-in-waiting
on the occasion of the wedding of the Lord and Lady Shigura.
She was a "gift" from the household of the powerful Lord Sato.
She was eight years old;
her name was Mako.

When her eyes met her lady's for the first time,
she felt as if her lids had been brushed with the silvery wings
of the great white moth.
She began to awaken from a dream.
From that moment Mako was always at her lady's side.

It was she who held the mirror when the Lady Shigura
attained the supreme enlightenment.
She who notified the chief administrator.
She who laid out the black silk kimono with the scarlet underskirt of
wild cranes.

During her twelfth year, it was said
Mako's rare and subtle beauty equaled that of the Lady Shigura.
In her fourteenth year, the first lady-in-waiting's
grace and charm were said to be as one with the Lady.
Lord Sato's son, with whom she had spent her early years,
had spread her fame to the capital at Edo.

In Mako's sixteenth year the Lady Shigura contracted a fever.
After many months she passed into the Void
on the full moon of the birth month of Mako's seventeenth year.

Each night since, Mako strolled in the autumn garden alone.
Tonight her steps were hesitant on random path.
Mako was feeling a deepening yearning;
yet Mako wanted nothing.
She trembled in the mountain air, having left her outer garment inside.

The shadows of the guests arriving to mourn with the Lord Shigura
appeared large and rippled, like puppets on the paper screens.

Mako's breath stopped.

There upon the path
was Taka Sato, looking fierce and fixed.
He didn't move:
Her step picked up. She came to him.

Dew, descending with the chill and the sun,
looked like tiny jewels scattered upon her smooth black hair
which hung freely to her waist in the fashion of the day:
the soft white of her silk kimono shone.
Lord Sato's son was covered in crusted mud and dust,
having ridden his horse and driven himself for an entire night and day.

It was said that
Mako experienced bliss for the first time when she was 8 years old.
Her burning desire to spend her life in retreat,
in temple life, was accepted as natural.
Except by Taka.

His burning desire—to have Mako his wife.

Lord Sato's son believed he had one chance
to interfere with the predetermined pattern of karma.
Taka was certain that he was Mako's destiny.
Childhood devotion, grown and flowered,
has the power of a thousand Buddhas.
He was sure of himself, yet unsure
if his arrival was too late to influence an outcome.

Mako appeared to be composed but was not.

"Too eagerly," she told herself,
she raised her face,
unaware of the effect as she looked fully in his eyes,
deeply searching for the unknown.

Her old playmate gave a whhf! of shock...
Her radiant beauty eclipsed the night's: gold of wafer moon, starlight,
last scent of wild violets,
bells, guttering candles, shadows mingling...

Taka Sato—was helpless.

All planned words, any show of erudite insights—gone;
it was he alone she now studied.

Mako's eyes widened.
Her lips, like a dusky petal trembles on the branch before
the final disconnection,
were quivering.

His heart beat loud and wild...

They stood, unable to move.
Entangled—like living marionettes whose strings the fates have
crossed—suspended, the tips of their fingers reach to touch...
the wooden bell interrupts...

Footfalls clicked, returning on the stone path.
Clappers called her to the bath but Mako hears another sound,
her soul—stumbling to know itself.

Lanterns along the path illumined not her mind's inner dialogue
but it's subterfuge:
her grasping, hidden;

her clutching, covered up;
her fear, paralyzing, of the ropes of attachment.

Mako has seen what pain that being human brings.
Mako knew in a sudden ripping in the painting of her happy life
that to truly attempt freedom, she must bow deeply,
not only to others' Buddha nature,
but to her own human nature,
she—like anyone else.

In the bath entry, Mako removes her robe;
her senses are usually quiet. Tonight
silken skin drinks the heat, full breasts pulse and round,
her soft hair against her waist brings chills, delicate feet
receive the uneven floor... all of her senses
vibrantly alive—awake—
as she had only known her soul could be.

He would take her love
as does the wild honey bird reach up to suck the nectar
from the far, far depths of the giving flower.

Should her beautiful body be forever unseen, unknown, ignored?

Mako stands on the step; she feels his heat,
sees his hands, muscled and scarred,
remembering his quick movements as he masters the horses,
as he looks…at…her...

trust…

a slow opening in her core...
a step down into the room which holds the waters and the coals...
Mako struggles to remain present;

each sound and change of air are magnified.
She stands alone in the thick fog of steam...
...mind's control of each little thing fades
into rapture. She
shudders, surrendering.

Devi, Divine Mother

Dark woman, draw near,
pace smooth and certain, like a queen.
You arrive from your ancient world
appearing as a simple girl
face in sun and light concealed.

Morning doves sweep upward.
Noontime bells are stilled.
Your gentle voice rings out
in villages and towns for miles
outside cathedral gate.
Ecstatic sound reveals a way to
what cannot be talked about in words.

Your song is sound's intoxication,
its dusky green embrace
a spell that floods along the trails,
soars in cataracts towards the
waiting fields and pools below
and calls all to come to dine and drink
your luscious feast.

Children move in uncoordinated dance
bump against your slender frame and laugh,
lie down, pretend to be
pebbles in a mountain stream
letting water-music cradle them
as when they waited to be born.

Tenderly the mothers
bend like lilies down to
touch the children's
wispy curls and tendrils.
They stand nearby

to see the rounded eyes
plump tummies arms and legs
wide open to receive.

Unlike those babes who recent came,
the mothers don't recall the splendor
of the goddesses and gods.
But your voice, Devi,
reveals to them the longing core;

the smoldering need
the unbearable wonder
the kiss
prolonging joy   surrendering
the savagery of bliss.

The Clam

On a day when the moon and the tide are right
go to the pools by the sea at night
there in the glow you may happen to see
a clam in the rocks spread wide its wings
leaving soft body moist and exposed to
the warm salt air, to the silvery wet,
to the gleaming that flows through the waves like snakes
and the radiant clam in the luminous light is
stippled in silver and golden streaks
fragile...fragrant...
a jewel on the beach.

Mojave, California 1943

she is on a train
returning to
Baby
for whom
after two
days
screeching
not sleeping
a call was made.

fun cut short.
not wanting
Baby
or Baby's puke.

wondering why
did I
marry?

she could pretend
not to have heard
static had ruined
had scratched the words.

"come back…she cries all day"
"what?"
"isn't sleeping…"
"I can't hear…"
"she is needing'
"she'll get over it"
'you'
"can't hear"
"what kind of mother…"
"crying's not…"

"are you?"

silver moon spills
on scraggly brush
night desert glistens with gains and loss
songs of the owls and the bats and the moths
brood in the rumble
of metal on wood
the clatter   the chatter
"come closer" "life's over."

"...and what about me?" the whistle wails
the words of her thoughts piercing the world...
all the work the
stockings the hat she
clenches her mouth her
chest is still she
glances down at her red high heels
then sits at the view with a surly stare
but there!
in the window!
is Baby.

spiraling spinning
she loses her breath
while little hands reach
grab at her breasts
little mouth erps
on her pretty new dress.

Oklahoma 1950

The boy looked up at his pa, quizzing his face.
Hands tightened each other's grip.
The boy strangled his cry, leaving throat squeezed.
"Yep," Pa said, real quiet. "Better git home."
It's too close the boy thought we can't.
His pa plain picked him up like a pup.
His run to the truck left the breath gone.
Nowhere to go, air dark yellow,
sticky honey.
"I'm hot," the boy yelled, as if it mattered.
He looked at the sky. Hollered.
Hollered again. " Pa—it's a big one."
Bodies slammed against the hood of the Chevy.
Pa's voice choked. "Go on, get in son."
They clambered to the side door.
Boy was crying now, saw the black wind rushing.
"Too close, Pa," he sobbed "she's gonna git us."
The father grabbed him like a mother will.
The sob broke over him as well.

12 in Love

My mind,
in contrary directions, spins—
and I would let it stop in any place at all
except the holy nuns tell me
that would be a sin.
Who are they to say?
After all,
they're nuns, not priests.
And so, I quietly decide myself what I believe
and thank God he gives us summers to be free.

This past one was just the best.
I didn't really eat and
hung around my house for weeks,
wearing shorts shorter than usual,
staying close,
not to my friends or mother,
but to the phone drinking tea
while fashioning a different style of hair each hour
the mirror chosen as my sole and dearest confidant
constantly affirming that I look okay or even better.

But then, tired of my bullying,
my confidant betrays
pointing out
my teeth
my ears
my thighs and other parts of self
are not alright or even worse.
Blame it on my size.
What's wrong with me? I am so slow to grow!

I turn to magazines for soothing
while gazing out the plate glass window

"my good mind wasted"
remembering The Day
when through this very pane
I saw The Miracle—
His Volvo Driving Up—
setting my body into deep freeze.
He got out and came inside
his hair slicked back just right...
so casually cool I could die.

But that only happened once.

So—flipping through the mags—
I admit I'm short on beauty
next to Sandra Dee, Audrey Hepburn,
of course Liz T, who I supposedly resemble
but that's a stupid way adults lie
to make themselves important
as if they are their own children.
Still, I do resemble—feel—like a cat on a hot tin roof
and yearn for the night when I listen undisturbed to Elvis
crooning to me that I am eternally turning him on
as he makes me weaken, blood cascading through
skin bones brain
waiting for The Call.

On the best nights,
I'm lying on my corduroy spread, alone in the privacy of new twin bed
and the phone rings and I answer like I'm so bored
and it's Him.
We talk for hours
on my softly lit-up princess phone
as I admire my legs in their short shorts
which enhance the poses in my new halter top

revealing, within allowed limits,
what has happened to me so well.
I'm laughing at his jokes, he cracks me up.
I'm lounging at midnight
sure this will go on 'til dawn
but then my mother calls out angrily
and just like a nun she
makes me hang up.

I love you

I love your face
framed in grey
the years lie there
the ones we share
the ones we missed.

You are dear
more dear to me than breath.
When I dream
at times you are young
at times an ancient one.
Yet, you,—Dear,
always the same
eyes filled with light
smile a boy's
you have no age
your true face shines
beyond our time
though you long to spend this life
with me.
What's most precious
is the love we have
for all beings.

You will do anything i need.
Your arms reach out
a still place in the storm
a trail ablaze in the wild flight.

Earthquake

I saw my mother in
strange forbidden nakedness
her soft slim body that
slips from the bath or
strips off a bathing suit gone
having nothing to do with this body now.

I knew I'd happened on a grown up thing
yet could not now retreat as
earth was shaking quaking instigating terror
of being swallowed up.

alone on the porch across from me
my mother stood
exposed
beneath a single swinging electric bulb.

She wore a gown of black transparent laces
designed to conceal as to better reveal
what makes us women, the private places.

I drew back repelled.
Although I tried to quell my snakelike glance
I couldn't tear my eyes away
nor stop the well of fear she stirred
 half clad, unbuttoned, hair unbound
strange yet like a girl she was
hands waving flapping warning

Then the earth gave another lurch.

Her hair was loosely down around her shoulders and her neck.
Her skin gleamed like butter in the yellow light
Her slim arms held away from her narrow waist

Brought out the fullness of her breasts,
as did the way the lace was placed,
In her smallness she looked helpless
clinging to the swinging rhythm of the earth,
arms stretched out from side to side
legs splayed, face white
not beautiful my beautiful mother this night
yelping and yowling like a cat and a dog,
do not "move an inch" she called
her breasts bounced and swayed
with the jolts of the ground
as mama forbid me leave grandma's house
by yelling   snarling
"don't move an inch"
Over and over and over again

Her child across the patch of green
wants all to remain as it was - unseen
I knows I must be the one to protect
my dolls, marbles, beading set,
the fake make-up and candy cigarettes.
The world of a child keeps me
happy in my room
tonight was becoming too close to the edge
where childhood ends and women begin.

so out of grandma's arms I slide,
into the smell of night I glide
past the tree with a fallen branch
around the rocks where fairies dance
over the moonbeams that spiders weave
the patch where trolls scheme to deceive…

My throat is choked as I try to gain the
wrapping of my mother's arms
around the pain of worry
that morning will arrive
before the rip within the seam
can be shown as small
and what I saw will be hemmed,
into the gathering dawn
then quietly put away

My heart felt a little like a coo-coo clock.
I would be punished for disobeying but
she was the one who had forgotten.
She had showed what was forbidden
not her clothes, but her naked need - I saw
her hidden love for me.

but just as I reached the stairway top
the rocking of the earth came to a halt.

I tumbled on the porch and watched
Mama straighten her hair, remove her gown
and stand there bare,
then reach into the atmosphere, still
thick and moist and dark.
Her bare arms, poised and raised
as if to clothe her specialness in air
began to dance to greet the dawn

Mama turned and saw I was there.
She gazed on me, the runaway
keeping her expression plain.
Then, like it was a pocketbook, she closed her face -
just snapped it shut -
turned away and went inside
without a backward look.

Ayurvedic Massage

Sounds of afternoon traffic
float near, just under the sill,
while hands
swift warm
smooth as green papayas
glide over
smooth curves
rounded mounds as
skin glows from within.

Am I the toucher or the touched?
The hands that pour
or the skin
that drinks?

Dissolving drowsing lazing
time slumbers...

A tap at the door...
ushers dusk
into this small room where I,
wrapped in stillness,
lie listening.

Her voice on the phone says
the car is new,
picked it up before school
did a few errands,
dammit what's next?
groceries are melting
cell phone is ringing
her child in car seat is sleepy.

Nails, wet, are tapping
anxiety streaming Mommy is
singing is laughing and...
singing to whom?
Mommy is rushing to...

Am I the driver or the driven?
The pleaser or she to be pleased?
Am I eternal or dying?

A Woman

they say she is together...

still...

there is an entire room
she hasn't cleaned
can't even find
her car's awash
in errands toys
cracker jacks pets

and yet

when she steps into a room
silence blooms

The Begging Bowl

I was with you, Lord.
I followed on the path you took.
You showed it to us all before you left
Telling me to join you at the feast.

I found myself upon the river bank.
The night was chill.
The moon was red.
I saw your trace though it was faint.

Breathing in your scent
I knew you to be near.
I slept believing you would wait.
At dawn I rose and was alone.

Lord, I lost that way I know!
The feast goes on without me there.
Although you've given me the key,
to turn the lock I must be she I am.

I passed my shadow on the road but did not say hello.
Her clothes are ripped, her skin is chipped, she
moans and pleads with leaves and trees and strangers.
"Where is my teacher?" "Who is my master?"

She thrusts at them her beggar's bowl and cup.
They shove them—empty—back and she looks up.
My worried eyes meet her exotic ones.
She alone must find a path to home.

Although I sing in joy each day
I miss her voice within the song;
Her footsteps cross the porch.

I open wide the door.
And thus I found the way, my Lord.
The feast was never hidden, it was forsaken
when I gave up what I witnessed
that brought pain and loss.

Your feast is everywhere.
I am content. I sit and stare.
You are so beautiful, my Lord,
…and rare.

Fathers' Day 1974

Like a robotic shaman bent over his work,
the chopper hovers above the wreck
its blades thrum a methodical hum
in this majestic Sea of Cortez.

The ocean's surface is grass green, flat like glass.
Air is settled, glittering, clear.
Its strong ionic field radiates a mysterious aliveness,
as do all earth's sacred places.

Coast guard pilots each easily read the history in things
bobbing as if in fun on this sunny morning.
Trash tells its story with
splintered antique panels
fishing equipment
beer glasses, shoes,
six life vests
knotted, buckled, empty, slashed.
Vests filled with men a few hours past
who had called 'til the end "may day"
"may day"..."may..."

My father was at ease with what he called the sea's madness.
Said he took her as she was because
he needed her vast peace, her primeval renewal;
war had taught him to plan on the colossal indifference
of the god supposedly available for emergencies.

His ship—just yesterday the ocean's paramour,
last night became its bitch.
The wind, too, transformed the ocean's soothing undertone
into a harridan's arrhythmic screech—
whining roaring wind destroying every bit
of shelter on that barren sea.

At midnight the ten men who were captured in
the sea's sudden tantrum yelled that
the time had come to give up.
Their final grief began, more terrible than any here had ever
been prepared to manage.
Men's grief...
in darkness...
curses vomit threats kicks
amid yellow flickers of the warning lights
to punctuate the mayhem that would hit in minutes
when the fathers would place their sons
in scrawny life boats plunged
into a black insanity of hope.

Someone had a gun; he had crazily fired at
shadows of a pack of carnivorous fish
careful circling—tightening—
"I'll be gone in time to miss the worst of it" my dad thought.
His mind measuring, as waves—twenty feet high—
pounded him down
battered his head and cracked the hull of his "second wife."

Strange.
He is numb
except for the taste on his tongue.
Of course.
Dust.
After all these years.
He feels the rage that never went away.
Oklahoma back in the 30's with its constant rub
in every folded place—eyelids, ears, elbows, crotch...
he had raged all right—then he met Phyllis.

244

He had never regretted it, marrying young.
He's glad now.
He can feel her breath upon his neck,
breasts still round beneath her gown,
her hair with braided flowers.

She'll want to talk to him for hours
about
losing him...
Will wait up...

The black waves curl.

A man who knows when to hold
knows the time to fold.
He slips between the molecules
not knowing where to go but back
into the way it was.

Smooth as a seal
he can move now anywhere at will,
but knows the journey will not wait.
A light ahead...invades his reluctance
leading him.
He can see it clear.
He loves the way he feels,
body gone but senses
filled...a spreading thrill...

without a backward glance
he soars into the other world.

Forgotten

Though my thoughts are growing leery, I
travel on in spite of weary warnings of the smatterings of
rain upon my head. And
though it is a sound that charms I
dread a bit the snapping
of the fire in the hearth at home, as
if it harms instead of warms.

Once through the door
I freshen my appearance up then
lay a tray with goodies of a day bygone—
scones and jam and Scottish tea—as
well as pull a biscuit from the drawer, for
man's best friend is woman's child who
must be fed for me to be relaxed.
Yet, 'though the lovely preparations, I find
my shoulders drooping in anticipation
of the evening alone.

But what a dunce I have become!
I had forgot the tome I found
yesterday as I perused the shelves in Oliver's
a big romantic mystery replete with interludes of forces
large and forces small, of history and herstory and traces of
philosophy.

Now my face portrays several new expressions,
one content, one well pleased,
and one most eager to proceed.

I laugh as looking down upon my
dress I see the dire shapes and shades I had
chosen for tonight's attire. "Poor Me," I thought,
"I had forgot how lovely is a book abed, while lost in

worlds of others making, the thrills and
turns of fate of late night heroes and their lovers."

Tea must steep, so
I will sleep in other clothes tonight... more
suited to the book I chose:
the silken robe, the tiny undies, a gown of
creamy white and lace
so well suited to my taste—a bit
rambunctious but with both charm and grace, I hope.
The mirror calls—I must admit I'm having fun
to see how fetching I've become.

Happily my tummy rumbles
Telling me
"indulge your British feast!
Raise your tiny well bred feet upon the ottoman
and lose your way in
food and drink—
and read!"

But I must think.
Did I forget?
Is this the night dear Reginald
returns from business trip?
I fear his early entry
will curtail my evening's activity,
You see,
when I read I'm quite simply irresistible
and sometimes I am scandalous
for I am so immersed in words, I am what
I am being in the book.

Therefore, tonight when he arrives
to find his love is lost in
tome I had perused,
I predict he then will choose to also lose
the every day and be my
pirate, prince, or master.

Then again he may
have hurried to my house with other ways in mind
to make my pulse move faster
until the pattering of rain above
becomes a rushy
roar of blood into my head and other parts that all
converge into my heart and it's desire...
How could I forget and feel forlorn
with such a man come to my home most every night?
Turn to books and eat alone,
act as if he'd not been born?

My therapist says I am simply scared as any
virgin in the novels that I so adore.
"Afraid?" I say. "Why no!
I just forgot because he'd gone
that he was coming back."

But to myself I will concede
I still awake in misery, in
fear and dread about my past.
That awful time.
Love didn't last.

Three Poems

I

Within me you live but leave no trace.
This feeling of you near
this joy includes
the unbearable fading of love.
Illusion of such great loss...makes me wake
again and again
before beginnings of day
to glimpse
brush strokes
of your beauty in
the silence and colors of dawn.

II

You Are Familiar, Lord.
Your body, for this moment,
is a carpeting of roses,
fragrant and wilding.

III

I laid my face to rest.
You came as light
lifted me to you
with rapturous cry
exploded the lies hidden in myth.
Lord, I no more have to search for you.
I simply open my eyes.

Satori

To be enlightened is to know the world as it is.

I have been enlightened.

You may wonder...
My answer is, it doesn't matter.

My enlightenment passed like wooden shoes over a bridge:
clattered along strengthened calmed
wood on wood...my god how long...
the happy clacking sound was gone.

The river below raged that night
the moon was blue and tugged at the tides
the hair the shoes and the dress were drenched
to the bone on the bridge on the fisherman's bench

Breath no thought
shapes then things
planning reasoning
analyze judge
"that over there is better than this."

I was weeping.

There had been no far side of the bridge
no arrival no departure
steps were dancing then slowed down
then stopped. Nothing else to tell.

I get up each day;
Though I am not the same I am
not
I get up and watch me move and sit and do

the chores of life.
There are times
I wonder what happened to my mind—
if I left the one I am behind.

My hand, relaxed, moves across the page like leaves
tumbling smoothly down a branch.
I glance up and see a bridge.

Paper crinkles in the shifting light.
I watch the ink. It dries.

Song of Sadhu*

How sweet the milk, clotted and sour.
How warm the embers of last night's fires.
The sadhu's gift pours out from his heart,
to desire what I've already got.

I wake. Silver moon fades grey...sitting...air pulsating...the hush.
Ripe. Ready. This fecund fertile quiet captures my soul.
Dawn's drum draws me down down down in.
My heart beats like a girl's as I enter the deep stream.

How sweet the milk, clotted and sour.
How warm the embers of last night's fires.
The sadhu's gift pours out from his heart,
to desire what I've already got.

I can't get enough of this wondrous world.
Age and decay are illusions of time; it's joy that is boundless.
But you, dear, must promise to stay...wow we'll not leave
until I no longer can move the pen in praise.

How sweet the milk, clotted and sour.
How warm the embers of last night's fires.
The sadhu's gift pours out from his heart,
to desire what I've already got.

*In response to a poem by Emöke B'Rácz

Girl No Longer

I
the wind was westerly

fear slipped under the night door
skulls dangled sliding amongst us
lights lowered and shivered
screens banged at the windows
dogs barked in the yard
beneath the sill a snake slithered
green top, on yellow it crawls.

unwelcomed   unmentioned

II
at dawn

fear's shadow
slid under my bedding
engulfed me put his hand in
fingers flicking wrist twisting
thighs warm wet
are told "be still"
I lay wooden—enduring.

alone   unprotested

III
the fear that came that night

he returned one full moon to mess with me.
I'd got away four years now
had roamed, worked the earth—earned money...
one thing I learned was this:
every person suffers.

and women - some stay clear others
get up in the face of trouble but
all sorts of women are kind to a stranger.
I let him knock, kept the door locked

off guard   unprotected

IV
faceoff

so when I hear his truck pull up late summer
I say to myself "you're a girl no longer."
Right there and then
I call Ed and tell him,
all the mess—I'd never said...
then I get my courage, stomp to the porch,
shout real loud, "get the hell off—
I just spoke to the sheriff...told him about it."
He knew what I done.
But he won't run—he'll tell himself
he can outsmart this.

He's wrong   I'm smarter

IV
hungry ghosts

gusts blow pawing the night door.
Those four years I left
I battled fear—found
it's a fraud, not a guide.
So I open the door—let them creep in,
skulls clanging eyes begging
tell them "sit"; show the side of the stove—

ghosts and ghouls are cold in summer.
I offer a meal though it couldn't fill.
they only slurp on fear and guilt,
I'm not expectin' them back next year..

at ease.   unprotected.

V
the warmth of the spare room

Last night I made love
I took my clothes off
I felt that I could never love enough
see his eyes deepen enough
the film around the story of
body giving to body
peeled away slowly
as we joined
leaving colors simple bright.
My lover's hands in silence have gentled the past.
My lover's love has shown me
others can be lights for us
as we find our way.

A Tea Ceremony

ah! the swift swish clack of the whisk.
green foam
froths
honored guest
contemplates
cracked teapot.

old chilled bones,
deep winter's inconvenience,
he has vowed to ignore
for more important
thoughts of
pots's impermanence.

he sits
impatient but determined

he's heard
no-self
can emerge
in a tea ceremony.

one last wish he
hopes to buy
before the end.

at last—begin.

the Mistress of Tea
rises to her knees.
she is
a beginner
who muddled through
the wisk and now must pour.

the heated water falls from the spout.
she gasps.
thinks
"My first mistake. But not too bad."

As tea's steam
leaps
divides on air's ice
floats
re-merges
the moment erases distinction's illusion
of two
erasing ambition's illusion
of one.

how fortuitous!

but alas...
old bones draped in silken robes
must nap
as
sun reaches crest to begin its downward path.

grumpy guest
mouth turned down
bows
polite but peeved
muttering—he leaves
"once more—a bore—
why keep trying a tea ceremony?"

his retainer waits
his face is smooth as river pebbles
"Of course," he thinks "because you are too cheap to get the real
thing,"
but this retainer has one eye on the mistress of tea.

the priest who runs the temple
listens.
he is trapped siting in the lead at late morning meditation.
he imagines his ledger without the tithing of this patron of zen.
he nods at the accountant who sits nearby with open eyes.
the accountant slightly shrugs, gets up, goes out.
"What can I do?" he thinks. "You can't enlighten old fools."
He brightens as he sees the mistress of tea's student ready to leave.

Who notices the little nun who comes each day to wash the latrines,
clean the priests' study, the meditation hall and
cook for them all?

it is she who watches.

EAVAN BOLAND, LISEL MUELLER, SAPPHO, WISLAWA SZYM-
BORSKA, EMILY DICKINSON, CHARLOTTE MEW, ANNA
AKHMATOVA, KATALIN LADIK, CATHY SMITH BOWERS, KATH-
RYN STRIPLING BYER, JIMMIE MARGARET GILLIAM, JANICE
MOORE FULLER, PAT RIVIERE-SEEL, MAYA ANGELOU, SHA-
RON OLDS, SYLVIA PLATH, ADRIENNE RICH, JUDY GRAHN,
LINDA GREGG, MARIE HOWE, ELLEN BRYANT VOIGHT,
HEATHER McHUGH, EDNA ST VINCENT MILLAY, ELIZABETH
BISHOP, H.D., ELENI FORTUNI, DERORA BERNSTEIN, DO-
REEN STOCK, TESS GALLAGHER, NELLY SACHS, CAROL LEE
SANCHEZ, PAULA GUN ALLEN, MARGE PIERCY, CAROLYN
FORCHÉ, GWENDOLYN BROOKS, DENISE LEVERTOV, NIKKI
GIOVANNI, MARY OLIVER, RUTH STONE, HONOR MOORE, MI-
RABAI, MARYLIN HACKER, CHRISTINA ROSETTI, JUNE JOR-
DAN, bel hooks, STEVIE SMITH, DARA WIER, GERTRUDE STEIN

CPSIA information can be obtained at www.ICGtesting.com
Printed in the USA
BVOW021821240613

324132BV00005B/15/P